FONDUE
& raclette

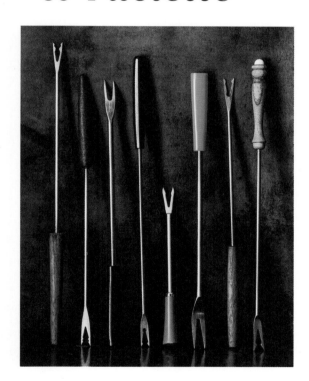

FONDUE
& raclette

INDULGENT RECIPES FOR MELTED
CHEESE, STOCK POTS & MORE

LOUISE PICKFORD

photography by
IAN WALLACE

RYLAND PETERS & SMALL
LONDON • NEW YORK

Senior Designer Toni Kay
Senior Editor Gillian Haslam
Editorial Director Julia Charles
Head of Production Patricia Harrington
Production Manager Gordana Simakovic
Creative Director Leslie Harrington

Food and Prop Stylist Louise Pickford
Indexer Hilary Bird

First published in 2022 by
Ryland Peters & Small
20–21 Jockey's Fields
London WC1R 4BW
and
341 E 116th St
New York NY 10029
www.rylandpeters.com

10 9 8 7 6 5 4 3 2 1

Text copyright © Louise Pickford 2022
(see also page 176)
Design and photographs copyright
© Ryland Peters & Small 2022

ISBN: 978-1-78879-472-5

A CIP record for this book is available from the British Library.

US Library of Congress cataloging-in-publication data has been applied for.

Printed and bound in China

NOTES
• Both American (Imperial plus US cups) and British (Metric) measurements and ingredients are included in these recipes for your convenience; however, it is important to work with one set of measurements and not alternate between the two within a recipe.

• All spoon measurements are level unless otherwise specified.
• All eggs are large (US) or medium (UK), unless specified as large, in which case US extra-large should be used. Uncooked or partially cooked eggs should not be served to the very old, frail, young children, pregnant women or those with compromised immune systems.
• When a recipe calls for the zest of citrus fruit, buy unwaxed fruit and wash well before using. If you can only find treated fruit, scrub well in warm soapy water before using.
• Ovens should be preheated to the specified températures. We recommend using an oven thermometer. If using a fan-assisted oven, adjust temperatures according to the manufacturer's instructions.

CONTENTS

Introduction 6

Classic cheese fondue 10

Modern fondue 34

Cheesy melts 56

Raclette 80

Oil fondue 104

Stock fondue 130

Sweet fondue 152

Index 174
Acknowledgments 176

INTRODUCTION

Fondues, and the concept of food sharing, gained huge popularity during the 60s and 70s, and I have many fond memories of evenings spent eating, drinking, laughing and sharing stories around a large pot of melted cheese. On the following pages, however, you will discover there is so much more to fondues than cheese, with a wonderful range of oil- and stock-based fondues, chocolate and other sweet fondues, as well as a chapter dedicated to the lesser known, but equally delicious and versatile, raclette.

Despite many versions of how the modern fondue came to be, one thing is certain – the sharing of melted cheese around a communal pot has taken place for centuries. On the slopes of the Swiss Alps during the cold months shepherds would dunk their bread in cheese warmed over a fire. The word itself stems from the French word 'fondre' meaning 'to melt', not surprising as France is just a hop, skip or ski over the border and the French are equally happy

to lay claim to the dish. Recipes began appearing in the 18th century and specialist fondue, and later raclette, restaurants soon followed. Today both are a staple on ski-resort menus the world over.

Oil fondues share a similar story, but with pots of oil heated over the campfire by Swiss herders so that skewers of meat could be cooked. This dish was known as Fondue Bourguignon, with the beef likely coming from Burgundy in France. It is entirely possible that it was the French who named the dish.

Stock fondues or hotpots can be traced to Asia, with the cooking method introduced into northern China by nomadic Mongolian herders who used their helmets as cooking pots over the campfire. The Chinese adapted the original dish and its popularity as a cooking method spread countrywide and eventually beyond. A hotpot is also referred to as a steamboat in some places, especially China, due to the unique shape of the cooking vessel.

Raclette, unlike a fondue, is not something cooked in a pot, but a cheese of the same name, melted by heating it. Confusingly it is also the name given to the cooking device used to melt it. The cheese, from the Swiss canton of Valais, was for a long time only produced in Switzerland. Today it is made in many places around the world, including France and the US. Taken from the French word 'racler', or 'to scrape', the exposed side of a half wheel of Swiss cheese was traditionally heated in front of a roaring fire and as it gradually melted, it was scraped onto awaiting plates. In the 1950s a raclette grill machine was invented, allowing restaurants and home cooks to enjoy the experience far more easily.

Cheese fondues

A cheese fondue is a combination of at least three ingredients blended together in a special fondue pot over a heat until meltingly unctuous and gooey. The success of any cheese fondue is the balance of both texture and flavour. It should be creamy and elastic but not overly stringy, with the flavour strong but not overly intense, as well as multilayered. Swiss and French cheese fondues are very similar and usually differ only by which cheese(s) are used.

Only three ingredients are essential: cheese, a liquid and some starch. In order for cheese to melt smoothly in liquid there must be some acidity. As a cheese ripens with age, its level of acidity increases, so ideally use a cheese between 4–6 months in age.

Traditionally a dry white wine from the Swiss and French alpine regions of the Haute-Savoie would be used. Muscadet or a Chenin Blanc make a good alternative (avoid overly fruity wines such as a Chardonnay). Beer and cider also work well but for an alcohol-free option, use water with 2–3 teaspoons of lemon juice added instead.

The addition of a little starch helps prevent the splitting or seizing of the cheese in the pan. Plain/all-purpose flour can be added to the grated cheese. Cornflour/cornstarch or potato flour can also be used but must be dissolved in a little of the liquid before being added to the pan.

The Swiss add a slurp of kirsch for a slight sweet kick to the dish but as you will discover on the following pages, cheese fondues come in a wide range of wonderful and intriguing combinations.

Italy has a unique version called fonduta made with an Alpine cheese called Fontina with neither alcohol or starch added. Rather, milk is used to melt the cheese in a double boiler, then butter and egg yolks are gradually beaten in to thicken the sauce as it gently heats. The result is a wonderfully creamy and rich sauce, but it can be a little tricky to manage.

Traditionally cheese fondues are served simply, with bread, boiled potatoes, cornichons and maybe a few slices of ham or charcuterie. But that is only the beginning and hopefully this book will open the door to a brand new world of fondues.

Cheese types

The classic cheese fondue is a combination of a semi-hard cow's milk cheese, traditionally Swiss Gruyère or Emmental, along with a stronger flavoured cheese, maybe a French Comté or mature Beaufort or English Cheddar. These are often blended with a creamy, semi-soft cheese such as Reblochon or Taleggio. I give options for what to substitute in most recipes. There are no hard and fast rules here and you can use one, two, three or even four types of different cheese.

Tips

- Unless you use an electric fondue, I recommend you make the fondue in the fondue pan on a stovetop and transfer it to the tabletop burner once it is ready; this will save time and energy and keep it gently bubbling.
- Avoid ready grated cheeses as they are often harder to melt. I use the fine side of the cheese grater for cheeses that are hard enough to grate. Finely dice or crumble softer, creamier cheeses.
- Bring the liquid to the boil before you start adding the grated cheese a handful at a time and stir with a silicone whisk or wooden spoon. Make sure you melt each addition of cheese before adding the next.
- Have a little lemon juice to hand and whisk in 2–3 teaspoons if the mixture begins to separate or split. If added in time it should help. If not, then sadly you will need to start afresh with new ingredients.
- The fondue is ready when all the cheese is melted, the sauce is thick and gloopy and will easily cling to a piece of bread dipped into and extracted on a skewer.

Oil fondues

Vegetable or sunflower oil is heated in a pan and diners skewer ingredients to fry in the hot oil. Born from the original Fondue Bourguignon (see page 6), oil fondues are now international in flavour and accommodate almost any combination of ingredients threaded or speared onto skewers and cooked in the oil once it reaches its optimum temperature (the success of a fondue is ensuring the oil is hot enough to cook the food safely). Most ingredients cook fairly quickly, in 2–4 minutes. Preparation of meat and fish is important with different marinades or rubs to add flavour and serve a range of dips, sauces and accompaniments with the fried ingredients.

I recommend using an electric fondue – they are sturdy and stable with an inbuilt thermometer to keep the oil at the correct temperature to ensure the food, particularly meat, is cooked through safely.

Tips
- Prepare everything ahead of time ready to cook.
- Invest in a sugar/candy thermometer to ensure the correct temperature for deep-frying is reached (180°C/350°F). Test the oil temperature with a small cube of bread – once in the oil it should start to bubble immediately and take 20–30 seconds to crisp.
- A meat probe is useful to ensure chicken or pork is cooked thoroughly. Chicken is cooked when the internal temperature reaches a minimum of 75°C/167°F and pork a little lower at 71°C/160°F.
- Heat the oil in your fondue pan on the stovetop to save time, but be careful when carrying hot oil to the table.
- Only ever put enough oil in your pan to come one third of the way up, so the oil will not spill over at any point.
- Only cook one type of food at a time (ie cook meat separately from fish or veg) to ensure even cooking.
- Change the oil after each use as it can easily taint your next dish, allowing the oil to cool completely before disposing of it somewhere environmentally safe.

Stock fondues

My favourite type of fondue is a hotpot or steamboat. The success of this type of fondue will be determined by the flavour of the liquid itself – the flavour will increase the more you cook in it. There is little to distinguish hotpots from steamboats other than the type of cooking vessel used to cook the broth. The hotpot is a saucepan-shaped pot that can be cooked either over a burner or can be electric, with its own heat source. A steamboat is the name given to the doughnut-shaped pot, where a ring sits around a central chimney. The heat source sits at the base of the chimney and is some type of burner. However, any fondue pot can be used, or even a saucepan, as long as you have a heat source on the tabletop.

Popular throughout south-east Asia, stock fondues provide wonderful banquet-style meals with tables laden with meat, fish, vegetables, noodles and aromatics. Versions are found around the world and any food that can be poached may be cooked this way.

Tips
- Prepare everything ahead of time ready to cook.
- Start with items that take the most time to cook, such as pieces of meat or bigger shellfish like lobster or crab, working through to those that cook quickly, like thinly sliced meats, delicate fish, veggies and noodles.
- Prepare the stock on the stovetop and keep or return it to boiling point before transferring it, taking great care not to spill any, to the tabletop burner.
- Keep the stock at a constant simmer as you cook the ingredients. A meat probe is useful to ensure meat or poultry are safely cooked through (see left).
- The flavourful stock can be eaten with or after everything else. It also makes the perfect base for a soup or sauce for another dish. Allow the stock to cool, then chill or freeze.

The fondue pan

You can use any type of fondue pan for these recipes, although I recommend a specific chocolate fondue pan, usually ceramic, for delicate sweet sauces. I use an electric fondue which is excellent for all types of fondue. Other fondue pans sit on a trivet or stand above the burner that provides the heat to keep the sauce bubbling. However, if you have a saucepan and a portable heat source, you're set to go.

Fondue skewers come with fondue pots, often colour coded so diners keep the same skewer throughout the meal. Small bamboo skewers can be cute for sweet fondues. Some fondues come with a set of slotted spoons. I think these are essential for all stock and oil fondues so buy a set if necessary. A ladle is really useful for stock fondues.

The burner

The most universal non-electric heat source is the widely available stainless steel fondue burner. The fuel, a liquid alcohol, is poured in through a central hole and absorbed into a soak pad set under a piece of mesh. Always take care when lighting any type of fuel burner – use a long match or taper. Holes around the top of the burner as well as an adjustable lid help control the flame and put it out safely. Liquid alcohol is odourless and readily flammable. You must take special care not to spill liquid fuel, especially near other flames and keep it well away from the dining table or any table linen or clothes when lighting it. Do not overfill the burner. If planning a children's fondue party, always make sure an adult is on hand to supervise the burner or candles at all times.

Tealights under a small pan or ceramic bowl can be used for chocolate or delicate sauces.

Raclette

Despite the fact raclette originated in Switzerland, it has made its way into the hearts and homes of most French families. During the colder months every supermarket or grocery store will sell many different flavours of ready-sliced raclette, from plain, to smoked to those dotted with truffles.

Raclette is a high fat, semi-soft cheese with superb melting abilities. It has a mild but rich flavour. Only ever shaped as a disc or 'wheel' weighing around 3 kg/6½ lb., raclette has a distinctive reddish rind and very strong smell which mellows beautifully as it cooks. It is matured for 4–6 months. Other cheeses can also be used and I give plenty of options in the recipes. As long as you slice or crumble your chosen cheese evenly, you will have a delicious gooey cheese to serve with anything you like.

The raclette grill comes topped by a hot plate (on which you can actually griddle ingredients or keep things warm – see photo above right) with a slot beneath to hold two or more small trays called coupelles, French for 'cups'. Each diner takes a tray, adds the cheese slice and pops it under the grill until it is so well melted that it literally slides off onto an awaiting plate. Traditionally raclette is

served with boiled new potatoes, cornichons, charcuterie and bread but that really is the tip of a recipe iceberg as you will discover in the exciting range of recipes that follow.

If you don't want to purchase a raclette grill you can just as easily, albeit it slightly less conveniently, cook the cheese slices on a non-stick baking sheet under a conventional grill/broiler. This can then be placed on the table for diners to help themselves. At a push you could gently fry the cheese in a non-stick frying pan/skillet on the stovetop.

Tips

- Prepare everything ahead of time ready to cook.
- Preheat the raclette or your grill/broiler 5 minutes before ready to serve to heat up sufficiently.
- Always follow manufacturer's instructions before using and for how to cool, clean and store after use.

I have had a blast researching and developing these recipes and am so excited to share them with you.

CLASSIC CHEESE FONDUE

FONDUE SAVOYARDE

1 garlic clove, peeled
  but left whole
125 g/4½ oz. Beaufort, grated
125 g/4½ oz. Comté, grated
125 g/4½ oz. Abondance or
  Gruyère, grated
2 teaspoons plain/all-purpose
  flour
180 ml/¾ cup Apremont wine
  (or Alsace Riesling)
1 tablespoon kirsch
a little freshly grated nutmeg
freshly ground black pepper
rustic bread, cornichons and
  radishes, to serve

SERVES 4

Hailing from the Savoie region in the eastern Alps just bordering Switzerland, this French fondue is traditionally made with equal parts Beaufort, Comté and Swiss Gruyère. However, true lovers of authenticity would becry this and demand a locally produced Abondance (a semi-hard cow's cheese named after the breed of cows farmed there) which is similar to Comté. In a French fondue the wine should also be from the region, namely the locally produced Apremont, the best known wine from Savoie. Typical of the area, it is light and dry with floral and mineral undertones. If you can't find any, then try an Alsace Riesling

Rub the inside of your fondue pot liberally with the garlic clove, then chop the remainder as finely as you can. Combine the three cheeses in a bowl and stir in the flour until evenly dispersed.

Place the fondue pot on the stovetop and pour in the wine, add the chopped garlic mixture and bring the wine to the boil. Gradually stir in the cheese mix and continue stirring until it is melted and smooth. Allow to bubble away for a few minutes until the consistency is as you wish. Add the kirsch, nutmeg and pepper.

Transfer the fondue pot to your tabletop burner and invite your guests to spear chunks of bread and dip them into the cheese and eat with cornichons and radishes. Serve with either the well-chilled wine, kirsch or a tisane of herbal tea.

MONT D'OR
WITH BREADSTICKS

1 small Mont d'Or cheese, 490 g/
    1 lb. 2 oz., at room temperature
2 garlic cloves, thinly sliced
2 sprigs fresh rosemary,
    leaves picked
60 ml/4 tablespoons Jura wine
    or dry fino sherry
a drizzle of extra virgin olive oil
coarsely ground black pepper
potato crisps/chips, to serve
    (I've used crisps made from
    purple potatoes)

BREADSTICKS
300 g/2 cups plus 2 tablespoons
    strong white flour, plus extra
    for dusting
2 teaspoons dried active yeast
1 teaspoon sea salt
180 ml/¾ cup warmed water
1 tablespoon extra virgin
    olive oil
2 tablespoons poppy seeds
2 tablespoons sesame seeds
2 tablespoons freshly grated
    Parmesan

SERVES 4–6

Mont d'Or, or Vacherin Mont d'Or, is a cow's milk cheese from Switzerland, named after the mountain itself. Wrapped traditionally in a spruce box to help contain the flavours within, it is one of the world's most celebrated cheeses. Part of the reason for this is it is only produced in winter, meaning availability is limited which, as well as its wonderfully complex flavour, adds to its value. Eaten au naturel, you cut away the top rind and scoop out the unctuous centre, but it's all about the melt for me. Baked whole in its box, the cheese melts to a gooey, almost liquid perfection and is best served with breadsticks.

To make the breadsticks, sift the flour and yeast into a bowl, add the salt and make a well in the centre. Gradually work in enough water and the oil to form a soft dough, then knead for 8–10 minutes on a lightly floured surface until smooth. Shape the dough into a ball, place in an oiled bowl and cover with clingfilm/plastic wrap. Leave to rise in a warm place for 1 hour until doubled in size.

Preheat the oven to 200°C/fan 180°C/400°F/Gas 6 and line 3 baking sheets with baking paper.

Turn the dough out onto a lightly floured surface and knock out the air. Cut into thirds and then each third into 10 equal-sized pieces. Using your hands, roll each piece into a thin stick, about 30 cm/12 in. in length, tapering the ends. Place the dough sticks on the prepared baking sheets, brush each with a little water and sprinkle a third with poppy seeds, a third with sesame seeds and a third with grated Parmesan. Bake in the preheated oven for 12–15 minutes until lightly browned. Cool on a wire rack. Leave the oven on.

Line a baking pan with baking paper. Discard the wooden lid from the Mont d'Or box. Make lots of small cuts in the top of the cheese and carefully poke in the garlic slices and rosemary leaves. Pour the wine and olive oil over the cheese and season with pepper. Place in the prepared pan, transfer to the oven and bake for 25–30 minutes or until the cheese is molten, bubbling and lightly golden. Stir the melted cheese mixture until smooth, then transfer to a platter and serve with the breadsticks and potato crisps/chips for dipping.

CHAMPAGNE FONDUE

WITH PICKLED WILD MUSHROOMS

200 g/7 oz. Beaufort, grated
150 g/5½ oz. Brie, diced
150 g/5½ oz. Raclette, grated
1 tablespoon plain/all-purpose
 flour
180 ml/¾ cup Champagne
 or Crémant sparkling wine
1 shallot, finely chopped
1 tablespoon kirsch (optional)
salt and freshly ground
 black pepper
truffle oil, French bread and
 a crisp green salad, to serve

PICKLED MUSHROOMS
250 g/9 oz. mixed wild
 mushrooms, wiped clean
125 ml/½ cup extra virgin olive oil
100 ml/⅓ cup plus 1 tablespoon
 red wine vinegar
1 garlic clove, sliced
2 sprigs fresh thyme
¼ teaspoon coriander seeds
¼ teaspoon black peppercorns
¼ teaspoon sea salt

SERVES 4

Add a touch of class to your fondue by adding some Champagne or a quality Crémant sparkling wine – their high acidity levels make them an ideal choice for fondue, enabling the cheese to melt to a rich velvety cream. I like to think I can taste the difference too, although this may be just the added glamour of a good bubbly. Naturally you must serve the remaining bottle as the perfect accompaniment. The mushrooms, brined with a spiced vinegar, are a perfect foil for the rich fondue. Use a combination of whatever mushrooms are available, even button mushrooms are good.

First pickle the mushrooms. Cut any larger mushrooms into halves, quarters or slices until all are roughly the same size. Place the remaining ingredients in a saucepan with 50 ml/ 3½ tablespoons water and heat very gently until the mixture comes to the boil. Add the mushrooms and return to the boil, simmer for 2 minutes and then immediately remove from the heat. Very carefully spoon the mushrooms into a large sterilised jar and cover with all the liquid. Seal with a vinegar-safe lid and set aside to cool. Use as required.

To prepare the fondue, combine the three cheeses in a large bowl and stir through the flour and a little salt and pepper until evenly dispersed. Put the Champagne and shallot in a fondue pot on the stovetop and bring to the boil over a low heat. Gradually stir the cheeses into the pan and continue stirring until completely melted and smooth.

Stir in the kirsch, if using, and transfer the fondue pot to a tabletop burner. Serve with little bowls of the pickled mushrooms, a drizzle of truffle oil and some French bread and follow this with a lightly dressed green salad. Any leftover pickled mushrooms keep well for up to 1 month in the fridge.

PLOUGHMAN'S FONDUE

1 garlic clove, peeled
500 g/1 lb. 2 oz. mature Cheddar, grated
1 tablespoon plain/all-purpose flour
150 ml/²/₃ cup beer – something with full flavour
30 ml/2 tablespoons organic apple juice
2 teaspoons English mustard
1 teaspoon Worcestershire sauce
a few drops of Tabasco sauce
ham slices, pickled onions, cherry tomatoes, lettuce, radishes, spring onions/scallions, white country loaf, to serve

SERVES 4

Growing up in rural England when a pub meal was a simple affair and, in those days, a bit uninspiring, my go-to lunch would likely be a ploughman's lunch. For those who might never have come across this British pub classic, this comprised a hunk of fresh bread, cheese, ham and pickles, accompanied by an obligatory pint of fine draught beer. This recipe is a homage to those good old days of pub grub eaten around a roaring log fire after a brisk walk in the country. Use a mature Cheddar, or even an aged Cheddar (look for a cheese of around 6 months in age), but make sure it isn't too hard and crumbly.

Rub the inside of your fondue pot with the garlic clove, reserving any left over for use in another dish. Combine the Cheddar and flour in a bowl, making sure the flour is well dispersed throughout the cheese.

Place the beer and apple juice in the fondue pot on the stovetop and bring to the boil. Simmer for 1 minute, then gradually stir in the cheese mixture until melted. Add the mustard and Worcestershire sauce and continue stirring until you have a lovely creamy consistency. Finally add a few drops of Tabasco.

Transfer the fondue to the tabletop burner and serve with a platter of the ploughman's accompaniments.

QUESO FUNDIDO

WITH TOMATO & CORIANDER SALSA

100 g/3½ oz. raw or cured
  chorizo sausage
2 tablespoons olive oil
2 spring onions/scallions,
  trimmed and thinly sliced
1 green chilli/chile, deseeded
  and sliced
250 g/8 oz. Asadero or Provolone,
  grated
200 g/7 oz. Cheddar, grated
1 tablespoon plain/all-purpose
  flour
170 ml/¾ cup Mexican beer
1 tablespoon freshly squeezed
  lime juice, if needed
2 tablespoons tequila (optional)
wheat or corn tortillas and sour
  cream, to serve

TOMATO & CORIANDER SALSA
1 small white onion, finely
  chopped
freshly squeezed juice of 1 lime
2 tomatoes, finely chopped
1 green chilli/chile, finely chopped
2 tablespoons freshly chopped
  coriander/cilantro
salt and freshly ground
  black pepper

SERVES 4-6

I tend to think of Mexican cheese as an integral part of other recipes such as quesadilla or nachos, but Queso Fundido is a Mexican fondue. Queso simply means cheese and Asadero, the cheese used in this Mexican dish, is a mild, semi-soft cheese from northern Mexico. It is a stringy cheese similar to Provolone or Gouda, which could be used in its place. Monterey Jack would also work. Mexican chorizo is uncooked rather than cured, so if possible buy raw chorizo sausages, available from specialist food stores and delis. Cured chorizo can be substituted, but the rind on both types should be removed before chopping. This version is cooked on the stovetop rather than the more traditional oven-baked dish.

Preheat the oven to 180°C/fan 160°C/350°F/Gas 4.

To make the salsa, place the onion, lime juice and some salt and pepper in a bowl, stir well and set aside for 10 minutes for the onion to soften a little. Then stir in the tomatoes, chilli/chile and coriander/cilantro and season to taste. Set aside.

Remove the casing from the chorizo and very finely chop the meat. Heat the oil in a small frying pan/skillet and fry the chorizo over a medium heat for 3–4 minutes until lightly browned. Add the spring onions/scallions and chilli/chile, stir well and then remove the pan from the heat. Keep warm.

Pop the tortillas into the oven for 5 minutes to soften. Wrap in a clean kitchen towel and keep warm.

Meanwhile, prepare the fondue. Place the cheeses, flour and a little pepper in a bowl and stir well to evenly combine. Place the fondue pot on the stovetop, add the beer and bring to the boil. Simmer for 1 minute, then stir in the cheese mixture until completely melted. Add lime juice if the cheeses are not completely blended. Finally, stir in the tequila, if using.

Transfer the fondue pot on the tabletop burner and serve with the tomato salsa, softened tortillas and sour cream alongside. Scatter the chorizo mixture over the fondue and then top with all the accompaniments.

NEUCHÂTEL FONDUE

1 garlic clove, peeled
300 ml/1¼ cups dry white wine,
   such as Neuchâtel, Muscadet
   or Sauvignon Blanc
400 g/14 oz. Gruyère, coarsely
   grated
400 g/14 oz. Emmental, coarsely
   grated
1 tablespoon plain/all-purpose
   flour
2–4 tablespoons kirsch
freshly ground black pepper
crusty bread, cut into cubes,
   to serve

SERVES 6

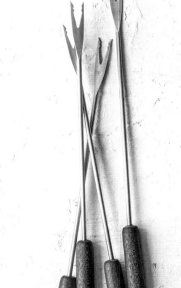

Neuchâtel is a lakeside city in Switzerland, close to the border with France, and its traditional fondue recipe uses a mixture of Gruyère and Emmental cheeses and white wine, with a dash of kirsch.

Rub the garlic around the inside of the fondue pot. Pour in the wine and bring it to the boil on the stovetop. Reduce the heat to simmering.

Put the grated cheese in a bowl, add the flour and toss well. Gradually add the cheese mixture to the wine, stirring constantly, and letting each addition melt into the wine. When the mixture is creamy and smooth, add the kirsch and pepper to taste, then transfer the pot to its tabletop burner.

Arrange the bread on serving platters. To eat, spear a piece of bread on a fondue fork, then dip it into the cheese mixture, swirling the fork in a figure of eight to keep the fondue smooth.

Variations
Other Swiss cantons created their own variations of this fondue, usually by substituting their local cheese and wine. Try it with your own local wines and Gruyère-style cheeses.

Fondue Fribourgeois: substitute 400 g/14 oz. Vacherin Fribourgeois, rind removed, finely chopped, for either the Gruyère or Emmental. Italian Fontina is another alternative.

Appenzeller Fondue: Appenzeller is a cheese washed in spiced wine or cider. Use 800 g/1 lb. 12 oz. instead of the Gruyère and Emmental, and a dry German wine or dry cider instead of Neuchâtel. Serve with bread, apples, pears, grapes and chicory.

Comté or Beaufort Fondue: these two French cheeses are big, rich, fruity, Gruyère-types, especially suitable for fondues; substitute 800 g/1 lb. 12 oz. of either.

Rosé Fondue: this is highly unconventional, said to have been invented by tourists in Switzerland who, finding themselves temporarily bereft of white wine, used what they had and came up with a funky pink version. Follow the recipe for Neuchâtel Fondue, substituting a light, dry rosé for the white wine. Not for traditionalists!

CIDER FONDUE
WITH PRETZELS

1 garlic clove, peeled
180 ml/¾ cup (hard) cider,
   ideally dry/brut
1 tablespoon cider vinegar
200 g/7 oz. Gruyère, grated
200 g/7 oz. Cheddar, grated
200 g/7 oz. Monterey Jack or
   Gouda, grated
1 tablespoon plain/all-purpose
   flour
2 teaspoons mustard powder
2 tablespoons apple liqueur such
   as Calvados (optional)
a selection of deli-style dippers
   such as dill pickles, salami,
   pastrami slices, to serve

PRETZELS
300 ml/1¼ cups warm water
1½ teaspoons dried active yeast
1 teaspoon salt
1 tablespoon caster/granulated
   sugar
1 tablespoon olive oil, plus extra
   for oiling the bowl
500 g/3½ cups bread flour,
   plus extra for dusting
125 g/½ cup bicarbonate of
   soda/baking soda
a handful of coarse sea salt

SERVES 6

Food trends come and go and cider has for the last few years enjoyed something of a renaissance. You can now find a whole range of flavoured ciders in your local supermarket, but I prefer to use a good brut cider, especially as I add an extra hit of apple with Calvados at the end. You could serve this with regular bread, but making pretzels is such fun.

To make the pretzels, combine half the water, yeast, salt, sugar and oil in a large bowl and stir to dissolve the yeast. Gradually work in the flour and enough of the remaining water to form a dough that is no longer sticky, but soft. Transfer to a lightly floured work surface and knead for 5–10 minutes until smooth. Place the dough in a lightly oiled bowl, cover with clingfilm/plastic wrap and rest for 30 minutes.

Cut the dough into 12 equal pieces. Roll each one out to form a thin sausage 40–50 cm/16–20 in. in length. Bring the ends together to form a circle overlapping at the top, then twist around each other once, bringing the ends back towards you. Press the ends firmly onto the bottom of the circle, a little apart from each other to form a classic pretzel shape. Cover with a clean kitchen towel and allow to rest for 15 minutes.

Preheat the oven to 200°C/fan 180°C/400°F/Gas 4. Line 2 baking sheets with baking paper.

Put the bicarbonate of soda/baking soda in a large saucepan and add 2 litres/quarts of cold water. Bring slowly to the boil. Carefully immerse 2–3 pretzels at a time into the boiling water and cook for 30 seconds. Remove with a slotted spoon, shaking off as much water as you can, place on the prepared baking sheets and scatter with sea salt. Repeat with the remaining pretzels. Transfer to the preheated oven and bake for 15 minutes until beautifully golden. Cool on a wire rack.

To prepare the fondue, rub the peeled garlic clove around the inside of your fondue pot and place on a medium heat on the stovetop. Pour in the cider and bring to the boil. Combine the cheeses in a bowl with the flour and mustard powder until evenly dispersed, and gradually stir into the cider. Continue stirring until the cheese is melted. Season to taste and stir in the liqueur if using. Place the pot on the tabletop burner and serve with deli-style salamis, pickles and the pretzels.

ROASTED TOMATO FONDUE

12 medium ripe tomatoes
(about 1 kg/ 2 lb. 4 oz.),
halved and deseeded
a small bunch of oregano, thyme
or marjoram (about 15 g/½ oz.)
1 teaspoon sea salt
2 tablespoons olive oil
175 ml/¾ cup dry white wine
1 garlic clove, peeled
525 g/1 lb. 3 oz. cheese, such as
Gruyère, Emmental, Vacherin
Fribourgeois or a mixture,
grated
1 tablespoon plain/all-purpose
flour
freshly ground black pepper

TO SERVE
1.25 kg/2¾ lb. new potatoes,
boiled or roasted
500 g/1 lb. 2 oz. cornichons
500 g/1 lb. 2 oz. silverskin/
cocktail onions

SERVES 6

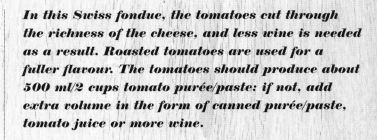

In this Swiss fondue, the tomatoes cut through the richness of the cheese, and less wine is needed as a result. Roasted tomatoes are used for a fuller flavour. The tomatoes should produce about 500 ml/2 cups tomato purée/paste: if not, add extra volume in the form of canned purée/paste, tomato juice or more wine.

Preheat the oven to 160°C/fan 140°C/325°F/Gas 3.

Put the tomatoes cut side up on a baking sheet and sprinkle with the herbs, salt and olive oil. Roast in the preheated oven for 1 hour. Remove from the oven, let cool, then remove any herb stalks. Transfer the tomatoes to a blender or food processor, together with any juices from the baking sheet. Blend to a purée, adding a little of the wine if the mixture is too thick.

Rub the garlic around the inside of the fondue pot. Add the tomato purée and wine and bring to the boil on the stovetop. Reduce the heat to a simmer.

Put the grated cheese and flour into a bowl and toss with a fork. Gradually add to the simmering tomato broth, stirring constantly, letting each addition melt into the broth before adding the next. Season with pepper.

Arrange platters and bowls of the cooked potatoes, cornichons and onions on the table. Carefully transfer the pot to its tabletop burner. Invite your guests to spear a potato on a fondue fork, then dip it into the cheese mixture and eat with the cornichons and onions.

BLUE CHEESE FONDUE
WITH WALNUT GRISSINI

125 ml/¹⁄₂ cup sweet white wine,
   such as German Riesling or
   Gewürztraminer
400 g/14 oz. creamy blue cheese,
   such as Gorgonzola or
   Roquefort, coarsely chopped
1 teaspoon cornflour/cornstarch,
   mixed with 1 tablespoon of
   the wine
black grapes and asparagus
   spears, lightly cooked, to serve

WALNUT GRISSINI
375 g/2³⁄₄ cups plus
   1¹⁄₂ tablespoons unbleached
   plain/all-purpose flour,
   plus extra for dusting
1 sachet (7 g/¹⁄₄ oz.) easy-blend
   dried yeast
70 g/2¹⁄₂ oz. fresh walnuts
1 teaspoon sea salt
2 tablespoons walnut oil

SERVES 6

Blue cheese and fresh walnuts make a delicious combination. This fondue is perfect served as an appetizer with grissini, grapes and asparagus. Alternatively, try serving this fondue as a dessert with ripe pears, cut into quarters.

To make the walnut grissini, put the flour, yeast, walnuts and salt into a food processor fitted with a plastic blade. With the machine running, add the oil and 200 ml/³⁄₄ cup water through the feed tube. Process in 15-second bursts until it forms a soft mass. Turn out onto a floured board and knead for 2 minutes. Put the dough into a lightly oiled bowl, cover and let rest for 1 hour.

Preheat the oven to 200°C/fan 180°C/400°F/Gas 6.

Knead the dough again lightly, flatten to a rectangle about 40 x 15 cm/16 x 6 in., then cut crossways into 1-cm/¹⁄₂-in. strips. Roll and stretch out each strip to about 30 cm/12 in. in length and transfer to a baking sheet (you will need to bake in two batches). Bake in the preheated oven for 16–18 minutes. Remove from the oven and let cool on a wire rack. Serve immediately or store in an airtight container for up to 1 week.

To prepare the fondue, pour the wine into the fondue pot and heat until simmering on the stovetop. Gradually stir in the blue cheese, then the cornflour/cornstarch mixture, stirring constantly until smooth. Transfer the pot to its tabletop burner and serve with walnut grissini, grapes and asparagus.

FONDUTA

½ teaspoon cornflour/cornstarch
250 ml/1 cup milk
400 g/14 oz. Fontina, chopped
35 g/2¼ tablespoons unsalted
   butter, melted
4 egg yolks
freshly ground white pepper
1 white truffle (optional)
   or truffle oil

TO SERVE
steamed spring vegetables
   such as baby carrots, baby
   leeks, baby turnips, asparagus,
   fennel and mangetout, cut into
   bite-sized pieces if necessary
cubes of fresh bread

SERVES 6

The Italian version of fondue is a speciality of the Valle d'Aosta in the north-west of the country. It is made with Fontina cheese, enriched with egg yolks, then scattered decadently with shavings of white truffle from neighbouring Piedmont. If you don't have a truffle to hand, a sprinkling of truffle oil will give a hint of the prized fragrance.

Put the cornflour/cornstarch into a small bowl, add 1 tablespoon of the milk and stir until dissolved – this is called 'slaking'. Put the remaining milk into the top section of a double boiler, then add the cheese and slaked cornflour/cornstarch. Put over a saucepan of simmering water and heat, stirring constantly, until the cheese has melted. Stir in the butter and remove from the heat.

Put the egg yolks into a bowl and whisk lightly. Whisk in a few tablespoons of the hot cheese mixture to warm the yolks. Pour this mixture back into the double boiler, stirring vigorously. Return the saucepan to the heat and continue stirring until the mixture thickens.

To serve, ladle the cheese mixture into warmed bowls and sprinkle with freshly ground white pepper and shavings of truffle, if using. Alternatively, sprinkle with a few drops of truffle oil. Serve the bowls surrounded by the prepared vegetables and cubes of fresh bread for dipping.

VACHERIN FONDUE

WITH CARAMELIZED SHALLOTS

2 tablespoons butter or olive oil
300 g/10½ oz. shallots, finely
   sliced
2 teaspoons light brown sugar
2 tablespoons balsamic or cider
   vinegar
250 ml/1 cup dry white wine
300 g/10½ oz. Gruyère, grated
1 tablespoon plain/all-purpose
   flour
300 g/10½ oz. Vacherin
   Fribourgeois, grated
2 tablespoons port (optional)

TO SERVE
bread such as sourdough
   or baguette, sliced and
   chargrilled cherry tomatoes

SERVES 6

Vacherin is a wonderfully flavourful cheese, found in two styles, both quite different. Vacherin Mont d'Or from Vaud in Switzerland and Vacherin Fribourgeois from Haut-Doubs in France are extremely soft and pungent cheeses which, when ripe, must be spooned out of their wooden boxes. Vacherin Fribourgeois, a firmer cheese, is the one used in cooking. It is not as sweet as Emmental, and so is a perfect foil for the sweetness of caramelized shallots. Substitute Fontina or Raclette if necessary.

Put the butter or oil into a fondue pot and melt over medium heat on the stovetop. Add the shallots, reduce the heat to low and cook for 10 minutes. Stir in the sugar, then the vinegar and cook for a further 10 minutes. Remove a few shallots and set aside for serving. Pour in the wine, bring to the boil, then reduce to simmering.

Put the Gruyère and flour into a bowl and toss well. Gradually add the cheese to the simmering shallot mixture, stirring constantly. Stir in the Vacherin Fribourgeois, then the port, if using.

Transfer the fondue pot to its tabletop burner, add the reserved shallots, and serve the fondue with cubes of bread and cherry tomatoes for dipping. Alternatively, put slices of baguette into 6 individual bowls and ladle the fondue over the top.

MODERN
FONDUE

PORCINI FONDUTA

500 g/1 lb. 2 oz. Fontina or
  Fontal, finely diced
300 ml/1¼ cups full-fat/
  whole milk
30 g/1 oz. dried porcini
  mushrooms
225 ml/1 cup boiling water
1 garlic clove, finely chopped
50 g/3½ tablespoons butter,
  softened
5 large egg yolks
truffle oil (optional)
salt and freshly ground
  black pepper
Italian-style bread, to serve

SERVES 6

This unbelievably delicious version of the Italian classic fondue uses dried porcini or cep mushrooms for their intense flavour, making it a year-round option. The dried mushrooms are soaked in hot water until softened, then chopped and added to the cheese along with their delicious soaking water. If you are feeling particularly decadent, serve it drizzled with a little truffle oil or even freshly sliced black truffles when available. Best served simply with a little bread, the fonduta could also be accompanied by a side salad.

Place the sliced cheese in a shallow dish and pour over the milk. Leave to soak for at least 1 hour to help the cheese absorb the milk.

Meanwhile, place the porcini in a bowl and pour over the boiling water. Leave to soak for 30 minutes. Drain the mushrooms over a small saucepan to retain the liquid, then finely chop the mushrooms. Place the chopped mushrooms and garlic into the pan with the mushroom liquid and bring to a simmer. Cook for 10–15 minutes until the mushrooms are really tender and most of the liquid absorbed. Season to taste and set aside to cool.

Pour the milk and cheese into your fondue pot and place this over a saucepan of just simmering water (make sure that the base of the pot does not make contact with the water). Stir the milk and cheese over the heat until the cheese is completely melted. Gradually beat in the butter and remove the pan from the heat, then gradually beat in the egg yolks, one at a time, stirring constantly.

Return the pan to the heat and beat constantly until the mixture thickens and becomes homogeneous. Do not allow the cheese mixture to boil at any point or it will curdle. As soon as it is creamy, stir in the reserved mushrooms and any remaining liquid, then season to taste.

Transfer your fondue pot to the table (do not place on a tabletop burner, but do use a heatproof mat) and, if using, drizzle over a little truffle oil. Serve with hunks of country-style Italian bread.

GOAT'S CHEESE & HONEY FONDUE

1 tablespoon olive oil
2 shallots, finely chopped
1 garlic clove, crushed
½ teaspoon freshly chopped
   rosemary
100 ml/⅓ cup plus 1 tablespoon
   dry white wine
200 g/7 oz. Gouda or a mild
   cheese, grated
1 tablespoon plain/all-purpose
   flour
300 g/10½ oz. soft goat's cheese,
   diced
50 ml/3½ tablespoons
   double/heavy cream
1 tablespoon clear honey,
   plus extra to drizzle
walnut or hazelnut oil, to drizzle
pear and apple wedges, walnut
   bread or grissini (see page 29)
   and celery to serve

SERVES 4

Pairing goat's cheese with honey is not uncommon and can be used to great effect in both sweet and savoury dishes, as happens here. With a hint of rosemary, this is great served as an appetizer. As with cow's milk cheese, goat's milk is made into many different types of cheese from super fresh goat's curd with no rind, through soft and creamy cheese with a soft, powdery rind similar to Camembert, up to a hard, crumbly aged cheese. In general goat's cheeses tend not to melt completely and are best combined with a good melting cheese like Gouda when making a fondue. I use a fairly young cheese here with little or no rind, but it isn't that crucial as all ages will work well.

Heat the oil in the fondue pot on the stovetop and gently fry the shallots, garlic, rosemary and a little salt and pepper for 5 minutes until softened. Add the wine to the pot and bring to the boil.

In a bowl combine the grated cheese and flour until evenly mixed. Gradually stir into the wine with the goat's cheese and cream, stirring until everything is melted and creamy. Stir in the honey and let it simmer briefly until the perfect texture.

Transfer the pot to your tabletop burner and drizzle over the walnut oil. Serve with an array of dippers, such as pear and apple wedges, walnut bread or grissini, celery and anything else you fancy.

SPANISH CHEESE FONDUE
WITH ROMESCO

250 g/9 oz. Manchego, grated

250 g/9 oz. Mahon, Taleggio or
Provolone, grated

2 teaspoons cornflour/cornstarch

175 ml/³⁄₄ cup Spanish white wine,
such as Albariño

1 tablespoon sherry vinegar

a mixed platter of Spanish
charcuterie, tortilla cubes,
bread and a tomato salad,
to serve

ROMESCO SAUCE

75 g/²⁄₃ cup roasted salted
almonds, roughly chopped

1 large garlic clove, chopped

75 g/2¹⁄₂ oz. roasted red (bell)
pepper, drained and chopped

2 tablespoons sun-dried/sun-
blushed tomatoes, drained

4 tablespoons extra virgin olive oil

1 tablespoon red wine vinegar

¹⁄₂ teaspoon caster/granulated
sugar

¹⁄₂ teaspoon smoked paprika

¹⁄₄ teaspoon espelette or cayenne
pepper

salt and freshly ground
black pepper

SERVES 4

Manchego is a hard sheep's milk cheese from the region of La Mancha in Spain, named after the Manchego breed of sheep. It has an almost unique flavour – zesty, nutty and fruity all at once with a slightly crumbly texture. It does melt well, although due to its somewhat grainy texture, I prefer to blend it with a semi-soft cheese like Mahon from Menorca if I can find it, and either Taleggio or even Provolone if not. Once ready to serve, I like to stir a little of the romesco sauce into the pot but the sauce works easily as well as a side dish. Serve it with a selection of your favourite tapas such as charcuterie, cubes of Spanish omelette or tortilla, crusty bread and a tomato salad.

First make the romesco sauce. Place all the ingredients into a small food processor and blend together until really smooth. Adjust seasonings and store in a screw-top jar until required.

To prepare the fondue, combine the cheeses in a bowl and add a little pepper, stir well. Blend the cornflour/cornstarch with 1 tablespoon of the wine and set aside.

Heat the remaining wine in your fondue pot on the stovetop until boiling. Gradually add the cheeses, stirring constantly until smooth and bubbling. Stir in the cornflour/cornstarch and sherry vinegar and cook for about 2 minutes until thickened.

If you like, stir a couple of tablespoons of the romesco into the fondue now. Alternatively transfer the pot to your tabletop burner and arrange the charcuterie, bread, tortilla cubes and tomato salad on platters and serve with small bowls of romesco sauce.

ROASTED PUMPKIN FONDUE

WITH CRISPY SAGE

1 x 1.75 kg/3¾ lb. pumpkin
    or potimarron
1 tablespoon olive oil
2 garlic cloves, bashed
1 rosemary sprig, bashed
2 tablespoons dry white wine
2 teaspoons cornflour/cornstarch
150 g/5½ oz. Cheddar, grated
150 g/5½ oz. Gruyère or
    Emmental, grated
75 g/2½ oz. crème fraîche
a little freshly grated nutmeg
30 g/2 tablespoons butter
a small handful of small
    sage leaves
salt and freshly ground
    black pepper
griddled bread, to serve

SERVES 6

The flavour combination of pumpkin, Parmesan and sage is a classic of course, but here it is taken to a new level in this fab roasted pumpkin fondue. You do need to choose a pumpkin that is roughly the same size as the one used here – a smallish pumpkin at 1.75 kg/3¾ lb. or a little either side of that would suffice. I used a pumpkin variety local to my home in France; called a potimarron, it has a chestnut flavour (hence the marron, the French word for sweet chestnut). Also known as red kuri squash, it has a thinner skin and less dense flesh than many other varieties, so you may find you need to cook yours for longer at the initial baking stage (test the flesh with a skewer – it needs to be scoopable).

Preheat the oven to 180°C/fan 160°C/350°F/Gas 4 and line a roasting pan with baking paper.

Slice the pumpkin and scoop out and discard the seeds. Drizzle the inside of the pumpkin with oil and season with salt and pepper. Pop the garlic cloves and rosemary sprig into the hollow, replace the lid and transfer to the prepared pan. Roast the pumpkin in the preheated oven for 30 minutes, test for doneness and then keep baking until it is just tender, checking every 15 minutes or so.

Once ready remove the pumpkin from the oven, discard the lid and increase the temperature to 200°C/fan 180°C/400°F/Gas 6.

Blend the wine and cornflour/cornstarch together until smooth. Combine the two cheeses and season with a little pepper. Spoon half the cheese mixture into the pumpkin and add the crème fraîche, wine mixture and then the remaining cheeses. Top with some freshly grated nutmeg.

Return the pumpkin to the oven and bake, uncovered, for 25–30 minutes until the cheese is bubbling and lightly golden. Just before serving, melt the butter in a small saucepan over a medium heat and as soon as the foam dies down, add the sage leaves. Cook for about 2 minutes until the butter is browned and the sage crisp. Pour over the cheese and serve with griddled bread. As well as acting as a receptacle for the cheese, you can scoop out and eat the roasted pumpkin flesh as the level of the melted cheese lowers.

SPICY SICHUAN FONDUE

WITH CHINESE PICKLES

250 g/9 oz. Emmental or Gruyère, grated
200 g/7 oz. Vacherin Fribourgeois or French Comté, grated
100 ml/⅓ cup plus 1 tablespoon single/light cream
a handful of fresh coriander/cilantro leaves
2 spring onions/scallions, trimmed and thinly sliced
crusty bread, to serve

CHINESE PICKLES
300 ml/1¼ cups white vinegar
200 g/1 cup caster/granulated sugar
1½ teaspoons salt
2 carrots, cut into batons
2 sticks celery, trimmed and cut into batons
10 radishes, leaves removed and bulbs quartered

CHILLI OIL
8 dried red chillies/chiles
1 star anise
½ teaspoon coriander seeds
100 ml/⅓ cup plus 1 tablespoon sunflower oil
1 tablespoon sesame seeds
1 garlic clove, crushed
2 teaspoons Sichuan peppercorns
1 tablespoon light soy sauce

SERVES 6

This intensely flavoured melted cheese dish is inspired by two recipes from The Art of Escapism Cooking by cookbook author and blogger Mandy Lee, @Ladyandpups. Highly skilled in her ability to fuse eastern and western flavours in one dish, Mandy creates dishes packed full of umami. Here a tempered-down version of her chilli sauce is paired with her equally yummy Chongqing melted cheese. The aroma given off as the chillies/chiles meet the melted cheese is beyond good and served with a simple bowl of Chinese-style pickles and warm bread, this is definitely in my favourite top ten dishes ever.

It's best to make the pickles a few days ahead of serving. Place the vinegar, sugar and salt in a saucepan and heat gently until the sugar is dissolved. Bring to the boil, then simmer for 1 minute. Spoon the vegetables into a sterilized 1-litre/quart jar and carefully pour in the hot vinegar. Seal with a vinegar-safe lid and set aside to cool. Keep for a few days at least before serving.

To make the chilli oil, place the chillies/chiles, star anise and coriander seeds in a spice grinder and grind to a fine powder. Transfer the powder to a small saucepan with the oil, sesame seeds and garlic. Bring to the boil over a very low heat and simmer gently, stirring, for 3 minutes until the chillies/chiles are turning brown. Immediately remove the pan from the heat and stir in the Sichuan peppercorns, set aside to cool. Add the soy sauce and store in a screw- top jar until required.

To prepare the fondue, place 2 tablespoons of the chilli/chili oil in a non-stick frying pan/skillet and add the grated cheese and cream. Bring the mixture to the boil, cover with a lid and cook gently over a very low heat for 15–20 minutes until the cheese is completely melted. You will most likely end up with a crusty cheese base, which is delicious when you get to the bottom of the pan!

Transfer the pan to the table and scatter over the coriander/cilantro leaves and spring onions/scallions. Serve with the Chinese pickles and some crusty bread.

BLUE CHEESE FONDUE

WITH POTATO FRIES

1 kg/2 lb. 4 oz. Maris Piper, Yukon Gold or King Edward potatoes
2 tablespoons olive oil
250 g/9 oz. Cambozola, diced
200 g/7 oz. Gruyère, grated
1 tablespoon white vinegar
1 tablespoon cornflour/ cornstarch
1 garlic clove, crushed
1 teaspoon freshly chopped thyme
150 ml/²/₃ cup light blonde beer
3 tablespoons single/light cream
salt and freshly ground black pepper
chargrilled bread or Little Gem/ Boston lettuce quarters, ripe pear wedges, to serve (optional)

PICKLED RED ONION RINGS
125 ml/¹/₂ cup cider vinegar
30 g/2¹/₂ tablespoons granulated sugar
1 teaspoon salt
1 red onion, thinly sliced
1 garlic clove, thinly sliced
a pinch of black or pink peppercorns

SERVES 6

As a teenager I spent many Saturdays in the beautiful city of Bath in south-west England. In a quiet corner just off the main street was a snack shop that sold crunchy, extra-fine fries with blue cheese dressing. This seemed weird and wonderful to me at the time and I have never forgotten just how delicious a combination it was. Use a mild blue cheese such as the blended cheese Cambozola, a Danish blue or Gorgonzola. The pickled red onions are a newer addition and work well. If you prefer to serve this as a more traditional fondue then go for it. It is also ridiculously good with ripe pears and wedges of crisp Little Gem/Boston lettuce.

First make the pickled onion rings. Place the vinegar, 125 ml/¹/₂ cup water, the sugar and salt in a small saucepan and bring to the boil over a low heat. Let it boil for 1 minute, then remove from the heat. Meanwhile, place the onion, garlic and peppercorns into a sterilized 350-ml/12-oz. jar. Pour the hot pickling mixture directly over the onion and seal the jar with a vinegar-safe lid. Cool and set aside until required.

Preheat the oven to 200°C/fan 180°C/400°F/Gas 6 and line a large baking sheet with baking paper.

Cut the potatoes into thin fries no more than 5 mm/¹/₄ in. thick and place on the prepared baking sheet. Add half the oil, salt and pepper and stir well. Bake in the preheated oven for 45–50 minutes, stirring from time to time, until crisp and golden.

Meanwhile, combine the cheeses with a little pepper. Stir the vinegar and cornflour/cornstarch together until smooth. About 10 minutes before the potatoes are cooked, heat the remaining oil in a fondue pot on the stovetop and gently fry the garlic and thyme over a low heat for 3 minutes until softened. Add the beer and cream and bring to the boil, then stir in the cheese until melted. Stir in the cornflour/cornstarch and vinegar mixture and simmer for 1–2 minutes until thickened.

Arrange the potato fries on plates or in bowls and spoon over the sauce. Serve with the pickled onion rings and some chargrilled bread. Or alternatively, serve as a fondue with the fries, pickles, lettuce and pears.

COMTÉ

WITH CARAMELIZED CHESTNUTS, RAISINS & HAZELNUTS

40 g/3 tablespoons butter
30 g/2 tablespoons runny honey
½ teaspoon freshly chopped
   rosemary, plus extra to garnish
a pinch of fennel seeds, bashed
100 g/3½ oz. whole cooked
   chestnuts
30 g/¼ cup hazelnuts
30 g/¼ cup raisins
2 tablespoons balsamic vinegar
1 tablespoon cornflour/cornstarch
1 tablespoon freshly squeezed
   lemon juice
180 ml/¾ cup dry white wine
   such as Muscadet
500 g/1 lb. 2 oz. Comté, grated
salt and freshly ground black pepper
nutty wholemeal loaf, cherry
   tomatoes and a rocket/arugula
   salad, to serve

SERVES 4

The region of France-Comté in eastern France lies between Champagne and Switzerland, bordering Alsace and Burgundy. A mountainous region, it is renowned for producing one of France's most famous cheeses, Comté. It has a slightly sharp but nutty flavour with a richness and creaminess in the mouth. It is a great choice of cheese for a fondue as it melts so well, and is the preferred cheese in most French fondues. In this recipe the richness is further enhanced by a compote of buttery, caramelized chestnuts, hazelnuts and raisins with fennel seeds, which somehow makes me think of Christmas.

Place the butter, honey, rosemary and fennel seeds in a frying pan/skillet and heat gently until the butter is melted. Stir in the chestnuts, hazelnuts, raisins and vinegar and cook very gently over a low heat for 5 minutes until gooey and sticky. Season with salt and pepper and keep warm.

To prepare the fondue, stir the cornflour/cornstarch and lemon juice together until smooth. Heat the wine in the fondue pot on the stovetop until boiling. Gradually stir in the cheese, then add the cornflour/cornstarch mixture, stirring until the cheese bubbles. Cook for a few minutes until thickened to your liking.

Transfer the fondue pot to the tabletop burner. Scatter over some fresh rosemary and some of the nuts. Serve with the caramelized compote, chunks of nutty wholemeal bread, some tomatoes and a rocket/arugula salad.

INDIVIDUAL SMOKED FISH FONDUES

750 g/1 lb. 10 oz. smoked fish,
 such as cod or haddock,
 skinned and cut into cubes
2 garlic cloves, crushed
125 ml/½ cup virgin olive oil
225 g/1 cup cream cheese
125 ml/½ cup milk
2 tablespoons freshly squeezed
 lemon juice
2 tablespoons freshly grated
 Parmesan
cayenne pepper
sea salt and freshly ground
 black pepper

TO SERVE
8 eggs, soft-boiled/cooked and
 halved
strips of toast

8 small ramekins, buttered

SERVES 8

In France, a brandade is a thick, creamy purée made with salt cod. With a few alterations, it makes a wonderful fondue. Because preparing salt cod can be a time-consuming business, this recipe uses a smoked fish – not traditional but still good. Serve it in a fondue pot or in individual dishes.

Preheat the oven to 180°C/fan 160°C/350°F/Gas 4.

Put the flaked fish and garlic into a food processor. With the motor running, pour in the olive oil to form a paste. Add the cream cheese and pulse until just mixed.

Stir in the milk and lemon juice. Taste, then season with salt and pepper (take care, because the fish is often quite salty). Spoon into the 8 buttered ramekins and scatter over the Parmesan and a little cayenne pepper.

Bake in the preheated oven for about 20 minutes until hot and bubbly. Serve with the eggs and toast for dipping.

Note To serve the smoked fish fondue in a pot, transfer the mixture from the food processor to the pot once you have added the cream cheese, and heat gently, stirring. Add the milk, then the lemon juice. Transfer the pot to the tabletop burner to keep warm. If the mixture is too thick, add a splash of dry white wine. Serve as in the main recipe.

GINGER & CRAB FONDUE

25 g/¼ cup toasted flaked/
    slivered almonds or 50 g/⅜ cup
    Brazil nuts
250 g/1 heaped cup cream cheese
4 tablespoons green ginger wine
4 spring onions/scallions,
    finely sliced
2 teaspoons grated fresh ginger
175 g/6 oz. cooked crab meat
crackers, breadsticks or Walnut
    Grissini (see page 29) or toast,
    cut into strips or triangles,
    to serve

SERVES 8 AS AN APPÉTIZER

This is such a simple yet delicious appetizer. If you can't find green ginger wine, use sherry instead and increase the quantity of fresh ginger to 1 tablespoon. You could also serve this as a dip at parties – just make sure the burner and pot are safely fixed on the serving platter.

If using Brazil nuts, using a mandoline or vegetable peeler finely slice them into shavings. Set aside.

Put the cream cheese and green ginger wine into a fondue pot and stir until smooth. Add the spring onions/scallions and grated ginger, and heat gently on the stovetop until bubbling. Stir in the crab meat, then scatter over the toasted almonds or Brazil nut shavings.

Transfer the pot to its tabletop burner to keep warm and serve with crackers, breadsticks or walnut grissini or toast alongside for dipping.

CHEDDAR & CALVADOS FONDUE

WITH APPLE RÖSTI

185 ml/¾ cup plus 1 tablespoon
  dry cider
400 g/14 oz. Cheddar, coarsely
  grated
1 tablespoon plain/all-purpose
  flour
2–4 tablespoons Calvados
freshly ground black pepper
crispy fried bacon, to serve
  (optional)

APPLE RÖSTI
3–4 potatoes, about 500 g/
  1 lb. 2 oz.
2 apples, about 300 g/10½ oz.,
  peeled
freshly squeezed juice of 1 lemon
1 small egg
½ teaspoon sea salt
freshly ground black pepper
1 tablespoon olive oil

SERVES 6

Potato rösti (pancakes) are a much-loved Swiss classic. This apple version, flavoured with the fiery apple brandy Calvados, is the perfect foil for a Cheddar fondue. Cheddar cheeses are traditionally served with apples, so it's an apt match.

To make the rösti, grate the potatoes on the coarse side of a box grater, put into a bowl, cover with water and let soak for 10 minutes. Drain in a colander, then transfer to a clean kitchen towel and squeeze out very well. Grate the apples into the bowl, add the lemon juice to stop discoloration, toss well, then squeeze out in a kitchen towel. Put the potato and apple back into a clean dry bowl, add the egg and the salt and pepper and mix well.

Put half the oil into a non-stick frying pan/skillet, around 23 cm/9 in. in diameter, and heat well. Add the potato mixture, press down with a fork and reduce the heat to medium-low. Cook for 10 minutes until brown, loosen with a palette knife, then turn out onto a large plate. Wipe around the pan, add the remaining oil and slide the rösti back into the pan to cook the other side. Cook for a further 10 minutes until cooked through. Keep warm in the oven.

Pour the cider into a fondue pot and bring to the boil. Reduce the heat to simmering. Put the grated cheese and flour into a bowl and toss with a fork. Gradually add the cheese to the pot, stirring constantly, letting each addition melt into the cider. When creamy and smooth, add the Calvados and pepper to taste.

To serve, slice the rösti into 12 wedges, put 2 wedges onto each warmed plate, and top with bacon, if using, and a ladle of the hot fondue.

CHEESY MELTS

FONDUE ROLLS

WITH TALEGGIO & PESTO

250 ml/1 cup full-fat/whole milk
2 teaspoons dried active yeast
2 tablespoons caster/granulated
    sugar
500 g/3½ cups bread flour
1 teaspoon salt
1 egg, beaten
50 g/3½ tablespoons butter,
    softened
250 g/9 oz. Taleggio, rind
    removed, cut into 16 cubes
6 tablespoons pesto sauce
    (see below)
milk and salt, for glazing

PESTO
50 g/2 oz. fresh basil leaves
1 garlic clove
2 tablespoons pine nuts
6–8 tablespoons extra virgin
    olive oil
2 tablespoons grated Parmesan
salt and freshly ground
    black pepper

MAKES 16

These rolls use a Japanese milk dough (shokopan), resulting in very light, fluffy and slightly sweetened buns. Here the dough balls are pressed into small flat rounds, filled with a cube of Taleggio and a dab of pesto before being reshaped into small rolls. As they cook, the cheese melts and mingles with the pesto so they are best eaten just as soon as they are cool enough to pick up and tear open. Great on their own as a snack, much like Italian dough balls.

First make the pesto. Using a pestle and mortar, pound the basil with the garlic, pine nuts and a little salt and pepper until coarsely ground. Gradually add the olive oil, pounding together until you have a paste. Transfer to a dish, stir in the Parmesan and season to taste. Set aside.

To make the dough, heat the milk until warm and place in a bowl with the yeast and sugar, stir well and set aside for 5 minutes until frothy. Sift the flour and salt into a large bowl and work in the egg, butter and frothed yeast mixture until it forms a sticky dough. Transfer to a lightly floured surface and knead the dough for 6–8 minutes until it is smooth but still slightly sticky (if it is too wet to knead add more flour, 1 tablespoon at a time). Shape into a ball, place in a lightly oiled bowl, cover with clingfilm/plastic wrap and leave to rise in a warm place for 1 hour until doubled in size.

Turn the risen dough out and knock out the air. Divide it into 16 pieces (each one about 25 g/1 oz.) and shape into a rough bun. Press each one flat to form a 10–12-cm/4–5-in. round, place a teaspoon of pesto in the centre and pop a cube of cheese on top. Carefully pull up the dough around the cheese and press the edges together to seal. Place seam side down on a large oiled baking sheet. Cover with oiled clingfilm/plastic wrap and leave to rise for 30–60 minutes until doubled in size.

Preheat the oven to 180°C/fan 160°C/350°F/Gas 4.

Once the dough is ready, remove the clingfilm/plastic wrap, very carefully brush the buns with milk and sprinkle over a little salt. Transfer to the preheated oven and bake for 20 minutes until risen and golden. Remove from the oven and leave on the baking sheet for 10–15 minutes until cool enough to handle. Serve warm.

CLASSIC ALIGOT

750 g/1 lb. 10 oz. floury potatoes,
  such as Desiree, Yukon Gold
  or Maris Piper
100 g/7 tablespoons butter
100 ml/½ cup double/heavy cream
300 g/10½ oz. Tomme or Raclette,
  grated
chunks of cooked sausages,
  roasted vegetables or
  charcuterie meats, to serve

BLACK GARLIC & PARSLEY PESTO
15 g/½ oz. fresh parsley leaves,
  roughly chopped
25 g/1 oz. black garlic cloves
  (see note below)
2–3 teaspoons balsamic vinegar
a pinch of caster/granulated sugar
3 tablespoons extra virgin olive oil
salt and freshly ground
  black pepper

SERVES 4–6

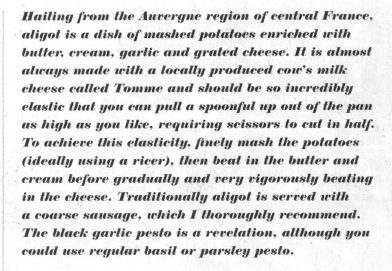

Hailing from the Auvergne region of central France, aligot is a dish of mashed potatoes enriched with butter, cream, garlic and grated cheese. It is almost always made with a locally produced cow's milk cheese called Tomme and should be so incredibly elastic that you can pull a spoonful up out of the pan as high as you like, requiring scissors to cut in half. To achieve this elasticity, finely mash the potatoes (ideally using a ricer), then beat in the butter and cream before gradually and very vigorously beating in the cheese. Traditionally aligot is served with a coarse sausage, which I thoroughly recommend. The black garlic pesto is a revelation, although you could use regular basil or parsley pesto.

Peel the potatoes, cut into chunks and place in a saucepan of cold water. Bring them to the boil and simmer for 12–15 minutes until tender but not mushy. Drain well and return the potatoes to the saucepan, heat briefly for several seconds, then cover with a kitchen towel and set aside for 10 minutes to steam. Pass the potatoes through a potato ricer or mash as finely as you can.

To make the pesto, place the parsley, garlic and a little salt and pepper in a blender and blitz until the parsley is finely chopped. Add the vinegar, sugar and olive oil and blend until smooth.

Heat the butter and cream together in a clean saucepan until melted and the mixture is just warm. Return the potato mash to its pan and place over a low heat, then gradually beat in the warm cream mixture until smooth. Start adding the cheese, beating vigorously with a wooden spoon until all the cheese is incorporated and the mash becomes glossy and elastic.

Transfer the pan to the tabletop burner for guests to help themselves, drizzling over the pesto. Serve with chunks of cooked sausages, roasted vegetables or charcuterie meats.

Note Black garlic is one of those food trends that comes and goes; however the process of a very long, slow cooking method has been around for centuries, first practised in Asia. The flavour becomes sweet and caramel-like, with a creamy paste-like texture.

TWICE-BAKED CHEESE SOUFFLÉS

WITH BEAUFORT CREAM

olive oil, for greasing
3 tablespoons dried breadcrumbs
60 g/4 tablespoons butter
75 g/½ cup plus 1 tablespoon
    plain/all-purpose flour
½ teaspoon Dijon mustard
500 ml/2 cups full-fat/whole milk
150 g/5½ oz. semi-soft goat's
    cheese log, diced
50 g/1¾ oz. Parmesan,
    finely grated
4 large/extra large eggs,
    separated
400 ml/1¾ cups double/
    heavy cream
100 g/3½ oz. Beaufort, grated
salt and freshly ground
    black pepper
green salad, to serve

8 x 180-ml/¾-cup ramekin dishes
8 x individual gratin dishes, about
    14 cm/5½ in. across

SERVES 8

If you are hesitant to cook cheese soufflés, this is the recipe for you. Found on bistro menus throughout France, the soufflés are baked, cooled, turned out and re-baked with a creamy sauce. This is one of the most delicious cheese dishes you will ever eat – magically rich but light. You can vary the cheeses, but I love the slight acidity of goat's cheese paired with nutty Beaufort in the sauce. Make ahead of time, then set aside until ready to reheat (you may need to increase the cooking time if you do this to ensure the soufflés are heated all the way through).

Preheat the oven to 180°C/fan 160°C/350°F/Gas 4. Lightly grease the ramekin dishes with a little olive oil and then dust the insides with breadcrumbs to coat. Transfer the ramekins to a deep baking pan.

Melt the butter in a small pan, add the flour and mustard, season with salt and pepper and stir well with a wooden spoon over a low heat until the mixture comes together. Continue to cook, stirring, for 1 minute. Remove the pan from the heat and gradually whisk in the milk. Return to the heat and stir until it comes to the boil. Simmer gently for 2 minutes, stirring, until the sauce has thickened. Cool for 5 minutes, then beat in the goat's cheese and 30 g/1 oz. of the Parmesan until melted. Beat in the egg yolks one at a time and transfer the mixture to a large bowl.

Whisk the egg whites in a separate clean bowl until soft peaks form, then fold into the cheese mixture until evenly incorporated. Divide the mixture between the prepared ramekins and run a knife around the edges to encourage the rise. Pour boiling water into the baking pan to come halfway up the sides of the ramekins and bake in the preheated oven for 20–25 minutes or until risen and browned. Remove the soufflés from the oven and leave to cool for at least 30 minutes.

Oil the gratin dishes. Run a small palette knife around the edges of each soufflé and turn them out, placing them upside down in the prepared dishes. Heat the cream in a small saucepan until it just boils, pour over and around the soufflés then carefully sprinkle over the Beaufort and the remaining Parmesan. Return to the preheated oven and bake for a further 10–15 minutes until bubbling and golden. Serve with a green salad.

PIZZA RING WITH MELTED CAMEMBERT

2 teaspoons dried active yeast

140–150 ml/9–10 tablespoons warmed water

1 tablespoon caster/granulated sugar

250 g/1¾ cups white bread flour, plus extra for dusting

2 teaspoons freshly chopped rosemary, plus extra for cooking

1 teaspoon sea salt

1 tablespoon extra virgin olive oil, plus extra for oiling and drizzling

1 whole Camembert

freshly ground black pepper

roasted vine-ripened cherry tomatoes, to serve

SERVES 4–6

There is not much I can really say about this recipe other than make, eat and enjoy! This is the perfect in-front-of-the-fire sharing snack. You make a ring of pizza dough and pop a whole Camembert in the centre, bake until the bread is risen and golden and the cheese melted and utterly delicious. Serve with bread or roasted reggies to dip, plus a glass of beer!

Place the yeast in a bowl, add 50 ml/3½ tablespoons of the water, sugar and 1 tablespoon of the flour and stir well. Let sit for 10 minutes until the mixture is frothy.

Combine the remaining flour, rosemary and salt in a bowl and work in the frothy yeast mixture, olive oil and enough of the remaining water to bring the mixture together to form a soft dough. Transfer to a lightly floured surface and knead for 5–8 minutes until smooth and elastic. Shape the dough into a ball and place in a lightly oiled bowl, cover with clingfilm/plastic wrap and leave to rise for 1 hour or until doubled in size.

Tip the dough out onto a lightly floured surface and knock out the air. Roll the dough up into a log about 25 cm/ 10 in. in length and cut into 16 equal slices. Place them in a ring around the sides of a 25-cm/10-in. cake pan or pizza tray. Cover with oiled clingfilm/plastic wrap and leave to rise for a further hour.

Preheat the oven to 200°C/fan 180°C/400°F/Gas 6.

Remove the Camembert from its box and place it in the centre of the dough ring. Score the Camembert in a diamond pattern and drizzle with oil, adding some rosemary sprigs and salt and pepper. Transfer to the preheated oven and bake for about 20 minutes until the bread is risen and golden and the cheese melted. Cool for 5–10 minutes before serving with some roasted cherry tomatoes.

TARTIFLETTE

500 g/1 lb. 2 oz. potatoes,
  such as Charlotte, halved
150 g/5½ oz. smoked bacon
  lardons
50 g/3½ tablespoons butter,
  plus extra for greasing
1 onion, sliced
1 garlic clove, sliced
2 teaspoons freshly chopped
  thyme
400 ml/1¾ cups crème fraîche
500 g/1 lb. 2 oz. Reblochon,
  cut into quarters
salt and freshly ground
  black pepper
chunks of bread and a green
  salad, to serve

SERVES 6

I had always assumed that tartiflette – a dish of baked potatoes, bacon and Reblochon cheese – is a traditional recipe from the Savoie department in the French Alps. It derives from the Alvaris in Savoie, where Reblochon originates, but was actually invented in the 1980s by the union of Reblochon producers as a way to help increase their cheese sales. A great PR success as it is pretty much embedded in the food culture of this part of south-eastern France and indeed far beyond. The Reblochon can be diced, sliced, quartered or left whole as was originally intended, atop the creamy potato and bacon mixture underneath. To be honest, I like it any which way!

Preheat the oven to 200°C/fan 180°C/400°F/Gas 6 and lightly butter a 1.5-litre/quart baking dish.

Cook the potatoes in a pan of boiling water for 12–15 minutes until just tender, then drain and shake dry.

Place a large frying pan/skillet over a low heat, add the lardons and heat gently until all the fat is rendered down in the pan. Increase the heat to high and fry until browned, then remove with a slotted spoon. Add half the butter and the potatoes to the pan and fry for 5 minutes until lightly golden. Transfer to the prepared dish, add the lardons and stir to combine.

Add the remaining butter to the frying pan/skillet and fry the onion, garlic, thyme and a little salt and pepper over a medium heat for 5 minutes until softened. Stir in the crème fraîche and bring to the boil, then immediately pour the cream mixture over the potatoes.

Arrange the cheese on top, transfer to the preheated oven and bake uncovered for 20–30 minutes, or until golden and bubbling. Serve with bread to mop up the juices and a crisp green salad on the side.

REBLOCHON PITHIVIER

WITH SPICED BLUEBERRY RELISH

5 sheets filo/phyllo pastry
50 g/3¹/₂ tablespoons butter,
    melted
1 whole Reblochon or large
    Camembert, 500 g/1 lb. 2 oz.
¹/₄ teaspoon poppy seeds
6 slices pancetta or prosciutto
crusty French bread and a green
    salad, to serve

SPICED BLUEBERRY RELISH
250 g/2 cups fresh blueberries
150 ml/²/₃ cup white wine vinegar
225 g/1 cup plus 2 tablespoons
    granulated sugar
1 cinnamon stick, lightly bashed
¹/₂ teaspoon mustard seeds
1 strip orange zest
¹/₂ teaspoon sea salt

SERVES 6

Reblochon is a semi-soft cow's milk cheese from the Haute-Savoie and Savoie departments of south-eastern France. It has a soft-washed and smear-ripened rind that is edible and comes as a round 500-g/1 lb. 2-oz. disc. Reblochon is most famous for its melting qualities, with a rich nutty flavour and it is essential in the making of tartiflette, a Savoyarde dish of baked cheese, bacon and potatoes (see page 67). The best thing about this delicious cheese is its name which comes from the French word reblocher, translating literally as 'to pinch a cow's udder'. Who knows, perhaps that was also the inspiration behind the 'laughing cow' cheese!

To make the relish, wash and dry the blueberries. Place the remaining ingredients in a saucepan over a low heat, stirring until the sugar is dissolved. Add the blueberries, bring to the boil and simmer gently for about 3 minutes until the berries have just begun to soften. Transfer to a bowl and then strain the juices back into the pan. Discard the cinnamon and orange zest and simmer the juices until reduced and syrupy. Pour back over the berries and set aside to cool.

Bring the Reblochon to room temperature 30 minutes before starting this dish. Preheat the oven to 200°C/fan 180°C/400°F/ Gas 6 and line a baking sheet with baking paper.

Lay the filo/phyllo pastry sheets in a stack on a clean work surface, brushing between each layer with the melted butter. Pop the Reblochon in the centre of the pastry and pull the edges up over the cheese, pressing them together in the middle. Brush the surface with the remaining butter and sprinkle with poppy seeds.

Place the pithivier on the prepared baking sheet, transfer to the preheated oven and bake for 35–40 minutes or until the pastry is golden brown and you can see the cheese desperate to ooze through!

Just before serving, dry fry or grill/broil the slices of pancetta or prosciutto until crisp and golden. Arrange the pithivier on a platter and serve with the blueberry relish and the crispy prosciutto, along with some French bread and a green salad.

THE ULTIMATE CHEESE TOASTIE

WITH BREAD & BUTTER PICKLES

150 g/5½ oz. aged Gruyère, finely grated
1 tablespoon dry white wine
3 tablespoons crème fraîche
65 g/4½ tablespoons butter, softened
4 slices sourdough or rustic white bread
1 tablespoon Dijon mustard
2 thick slices good-quality cooked ham
a crisp green salad, to serve

BREAD & BUTTER PICKLES
200 g/7 oz. cucumber (ideally Lebanese)
½ white onion
1 tablespoon sea salt
150 ml/⅔ cup white wine vinegar
75 g/6 tablespoons soft light brown sugar
½ teaspoon ground turmeric
½ teaspoon yellow mustard seeds
½ teaspoon dill seeds
a few black peppercorns

SERVES 2

What makes a good cheese toastie? Should it be cooked in a frying pan/skillet? Made in a sandwich toaster? In the oven? Wrapped? Unwrapped? What type of bread is best? Should you put the pickle inside or on the side? Serve it with ketchup? These are all pertinent questions to ask and the answer is…whatever you like. My favourite way is to start it in a frying pan/skillet and finish in the oven, ensuring a crisp toasted crust and an evenly soft and gooey centre. I like the firm texture of sourdough and a simple filling using a good-quality mustard, cheese and ham. Yes, it is simple, but believe me it is just right.

To make the pickles, thickly slice the cucumber and onion into 3-mm/⅛-in. slices, place together in a colander/strainer and sprinkle with the salt. Set the colander over a bowl and drain for 2 hours. Taste the cucumber – if it is too salty, rinse thoroughly in cold water and then drain again. Pat dry with paper towels.

Place the remaining pickle ingredients in a saucepan with 75 ml/⅓ cup water and bring to the boil, stirring to dissolve the sugar, then simmer for 10 minutes. Add the cucumber and onion and return to the boil. Immediately remove the pan from the heat and ladle the vegetables and liquid into a sterilized 1-litre/quart jar. Seal the jar with a vinegar-safe lid and leave to cool.

To make the toasties, preheat the oven to 190°C/fan 170°C/375°F/Gas 5.

In a bowl combine the Gruyère, wine, crème fraîche and some pepper to make a paste. Spread one side of each piece of bread with butter followed by a little mustard and place 2 of the slices mustard side up on a board. Spread half of the cheese paste over the mustard and top with the ham, then the remaining cheese paste. Pop the remaining slices of bread mustard side down over the cheese layer and press firmly together.

Melt the remaining butter in a large ovenproof frying pan/skillet over a medium-low heat and, as soon as it melts, add the sandwiches and cook for 1 minute on each side until lightly golden. Transfer the pan to the preheated oven and bake for 10 minutes until all is golden, gooey and yummy. Serve with the pickles and a crisp green salad.

BACON, LOBSTER & TOMATO TOASTIE

This is reserved for special occasions in my house – a posh BLT if you like. I think it's really quite decadent to make something as everyday as a toasted sandwich into something a bit luxurious and this has to be one of our all-time Sunday brunch treats.

4 slices smoked streaky bacon
4 chunky slices white bread
  (sourdough is perfect)
65 g/4½ tablespoons butter,
  softened
150 g/5½ oz. Tomme or Raclette,
  thinly sliced
150 g/5½ oz. cooked lobster meat,
  sliced or shredded
1 large tomato, thinly sliced
rocket/arugula salad with a tangy
  lemon-based French dressing,
  to serve

MARIE ROSE SAUCE
3 tablespoons mayonnaise
1 tablespoon tomato ketchup
1 teaspoon Worcestershire sauce
a few drops Tabasco

SERVES 2

Preheat the oven to 200°C/fan 180°C/400°F/Gas 6.

Make the Marie Rose sauce by combining all the ingredients in a bowl, cover and set aside.

Dry fry the bacon until golden but not crispy.

Spread one side of the bread slices with a little butter and the Marie Rose sauce and place 2 of them plain side down on a board. Top each one with the bacon, a layer of cheese slices, then a layer of lobster, tomato slices and finally the rest of the cheese slices. Top with the 2 remaining slices of bread, plain side up, pressing firmly together.

Melt the remaining butter in an ovenproof frying pan/skillet over a medium-low heat and as soon as it melts, add the sandwiches. Fry for 1 minute on each side until lightly golden, then transfer the pan to the preheated oven. Cook for 6–8 minutes until the cheese is oozing and the lobster meat is heated through. Serve immediately with a side salad of sharply dressed rocket/arugula leaves.

SWISS FONDUE FRITTERS

8 slices white bread, such as
    a country loaf
250 g/9 oz. Gruyère, Emmental
    or Tomme, grated as finely
    as possible
1½ tablespoons plain/all-purpose
    flour
1 teaspoon Dijon mustard
1 egg, beaten
a pinch of cayenne pepper
2 tablespoons dry white wine
salt and freshly ground
    black pepper
sunflower oil, for frying
sweet chilli sauce, to serve

SERVES 4

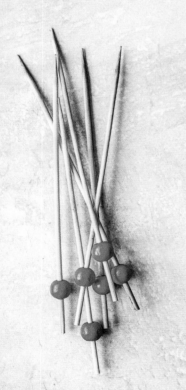

While researching this book I discovered a cheese fritter or beignet that I hadn't come across before – a malakoff from Switzerland, presumably originating from the place of the same name. Further research led to a definite lack of clarity as to the true origin of this intriguing deep-fried, dome-shaped mound of cheese on a round of bread. I suspect this version has been adapted by chefs from what is more likely to have begun on the hillsides by farmers tending their sheep, frying bits of cheese to sustain them during the cold months. I believe a malakoff fritter can also refer to a stick of cheese coated in batter and deep-fried. I have opted for this fancier version, best served with a glass of chilled Chasselas – a dry but fruity white wine, it is Switzerland's most coveted wine. You could also try it with an Alsace Gewürztraminer, but it must be well chilled. These are great as an appetizer.

Using a 6-cm/2½-in. cookie cutter, stamp out a round from each slice of bread. In a bowl combine the grated cheese, flour, mustard, egg, cayenne and salt and pepper and work together. Then stir in the wine to form a coarse paste.

Carefully place a spoonful of the paste on top of each circle of bread and using wet hands, shape the mound into a smooth dome about 3 cm/1¼ in. in height.

Pour oil to a depth of roughly 5 cm/2 in. into a heavy-based pan or fondue pot and heat to 180°C/350°F or until a cube of bread crisps in 30 seconds. Very gently lower the fritters, two at a time and cheese side down, into the hot oil and fry for about 3 minutes. Then flip them over and fry for a further 1 minute until they are golden brown (the bread base will always be darker than the domed top). Keep warm in the oven while cooking the rest.

Serve the fritters immediately with some sweet chilli sauce.

CROÛTE AU FROMAGE NATURE

a little butter, for greasing
2 large slices sourdough bread
1 garlic clove, peeled but left
    whole
75 ml/⅓ cup dry white wine
4 slices pastrami or ham, about
    100 g/3½ oz.
300 g/10½ oz. Gruyère
    or Emmental, grated
a little freshly grated nutmeg
2 tablespoons grated Parmesan
salt and freshly ground
    black pepper
crisp green salad, to serve

SERVES 2–4

*Directly translated into English, croûte au
fromage nature means simply 'plain cheese on
toast'. Definitely sounds more appetizing in French,
and it is more interesting than the name suggests.
It was, no doubt, introduced as a way to use leftovers from a fondue or just stale bread and cheese,
but here the bread is soaked in wine to soften it and
help the cheese, which is grated on and around the
bread, to melt more easily. Hugely popular in the
mountain regions it came from, it is a dish that
manages food waste and provides nourishment.
Ham or bacon and an egg are frequent additions;
I love it with the salty-sweet flavour of pastrami
and no egg, but that is up to you.*

Preheat the oven to 220°C/fan 200°C/425°F/Gas 7 and butter
the inside of a 1½-litre/quart baking dish.

Griddle the bread slices until charred on both sides, then rub all
over with the garlic and place in the prepared dish. Season the
bread with a little salt and pepper. Pour the wine into the dish
and top the bread with the pastrami or ham. Scatter over the
Gruyère or Emmental, some grated nutmeg and the Parmesan.
Transfer to the preheated oven and bake for 20 minutes until
bubbling and golden.

Serve with a crisp green salad and a glass of chilled Alsace
white wine.

Variation If you like, serve the dish topped with a couple of fried
eggs, or for those who do not eat meat you can replace it with
some sautéed and seasoned spinach.

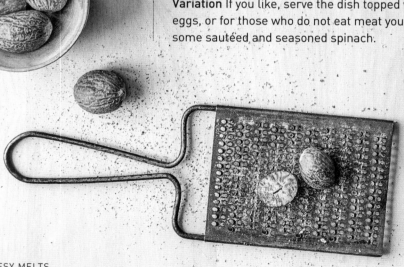

WELSH RABBIT

WITH MUSTARD ONIONS

225 g/8 oz. Cheddar, grated
15 g/1 tablespoon softened butter
2 teaspoons Worcestershire sauce
1 teaspoon mustard powder
2 teaspoons plain/all-purpose
   flour
a pinch of cayenne pepper
60 ml/4 tablespoons light beer

MUSTARD ONIONS
250 ml/1 cup verjuice or
   white rice vinegar (see note)
4 tablespoons sugar
1 tablespoon wholegrain mustard
300 g/10½ oz. silverskin/cocktail
   onions, rinsed thoroughly

TO SERVE
4 English muffins or thick slices
   of bread, toasted
grilled/broiled slices of bacon
   (optional)
blanched asparagus (optional)

SERVES 4

Nothing to do with rabbits, of course (you may know this dish as Welsh rarebit)! Many countries have a version of the perennially popular cheese melted on toast – French croque monsieur, Italian mozzarella in carozza, while this Welsh classic is a particularly creamy version. Do also try the Swiss version on page 76 – slices of bread layered into a heavily buttered dish, topped with a little wine and lashings of cheese, then baked until brown and bubbling.

First make the mustard onions. Put the verjuice or vinegar and sugar into a small non-reactive saucepan and heat until dissolved. Bring to the boil and reduce by half, about 5 minutes. Remove from the heat and stir in the mustard and onions. Let marinate for at least 1 hour.

Place the cheese in a saucepan with the remaining ingredients and stir well. Place over a low heat and stir until the mixture is just melted and forms a paste. Remove from the heat and cool for 2–3 minutes.

Put the toasted muffins onto 4 serving plates and pour over the cheese mixture. The rabbits may be grilled/broiled to brown the cheese, or left plain. Top with bacon and asparagus, if using. Serve with the mustard onions.

Note Verjuice – an acidic juice made from unripe grapes – is available in some delicatessens. If unavailable, use white rice vinegar instead.

RACLETTE

CLASSIC RACLETTE

100 g/3½ oz. Raclette,
  or other melting cheese,
  cut into 4 slices
200 g/7 oz. new potatoes,
  boiled in their skins
8–12 cornichons
8–12 silverskin/cocktail onions

SERVES 1

Raclette is an essential experience for all cheese lovers. Traditionally, huge half wheels of Raclette are heated beside an open fire. Periodically, the melted layer is scraped onto a plate and served with potatoes, pickled onions and cornichons. Nowadays, special equipment is available for melting the cheese, ranging from large grills holding two halves of a wheel, to nifty tabletop versions with little grill pans for individual servings. If you don't own one, an ordinary grill/broiler and pieces of non-stick baking paper work very well too.

Preheat the raclette machine, if using, according to the manufacturer's instructions. Warm all serving plates in a low oven. Arrange platters of potatoes, cornichons and silverskin/cocktail onions on the table.

Invite each guest to put a slice of cheese into one of the small raclette trays, heat until melted, then eat with the accompaniments.

If you don't have a raclette machine, heat a conventional grill/broiler until very hot and put 4 slices of cheese onto 4 pieces of baking paper, 12 cm/5 in. square. When your guests are seated and ready, grill/broil the cheese for about 2 minutes until bubbling. Using a metal spatula, scrape the cheese off the paper onto a warm plate and serve as before.

HALLOUMI & FATTOUSH SALAD

WITH CRISPY FLATBREADS

2 large flatbreads
1 large green (bell) pepper, deseeded and diced
1 cucumber (ideally Lebanese), diced
2 ripe tomatoes, diced
1 small red onion, finely chopped
2 tablespoons freshly chopped parsley
2 tablespoons freshly chopped coriander/cilantro
3 tablespoons extra virgin olive oil
1 tablespoon freshly squeezed lemon juice
250 g/9 oz. halloumi, drained and cut into 8 slices
a handful of rocket/arugula leaves

TAHINI SAUCE
200 g/¾ cup Greek yogurt
2 tablespoons tahini paste
1 small garlic clove, crushed
1 tablespoon freshly squeezed lemon juice
salt and freshly ground black pepper
a pinch of dukkah, for sprinkling

SERVES 4

Originally from Cyprus, halloumi, like feta, is traditionally made with a mixture of sheep's and goat's milk and is a similarly salty, sweet yet slightly sharp cheese. Unlike feta however, halloumi is never eaten raw, it is always melted and is a dish in its own right. Here it is paired with a Middle Eastern salad called fattoush, a combination of finely chopped salad vegetables, griddled flatbreads and loads of freshly chopped herbs, all seasoned with lemon juice and olive oil. I like to serve it with a creamy tahini sauce, which offsets the sharpness of the cheese and salad. Great accompanied by fresh mint tea, too.

Heat a large griddle pan or frying pan/skillet until hot and cook the flatbreads for 1 minute on each side until lightly charred. Leave to cool and crisp up, then tear into bite-sized pieces. Set aside.

Mix together the (bell) pepper, cucumber, tomatoes, onion and herbs in a bowl. Add the flatbread pieces and stir in the olive oil and lemon juice. Season to taste.

To make the tahini sauce, combine all the ingredients in a bowl.

Heat the raclette machine or a conventional grill/broiler to the highest setting. Place the halloumi slices on the raclette trays and cook for 2–3 minutes until softened and bubbling (they probably won't brown).

Meanwhile, invite your guests to help themselves to the tahini sauce, fattoush and rocket/arugula leaves. As soon as the cheese is melted, scrape or spoon it directly on to the fattoush on everyone's plates and scatter over a pinch of dukkah.

DOLCELATTE & SWEET POTATO SALAD WITH CARAMELIZED PECANS

750 g/1 lb. 10 oz. sweet potatoes
1 large red onion, cut into thin
  wedges
2 tablespoons extra virgin olive oil
100 g/3$\frac{1}{2}$ oz. pecan nuts
3 tablespoons maple syrup
$\frac{1}{2}$ teaspoon smoked paprika
$\frac{1}{4}$ teaspoon cayenne pepper
$\frac{1}{4}$ teaspoon sea salt
200 g/7 oz. green beans, trimmed
  and halved
100 g/3$\frac{1}{2}$ oz. baby spinach leaves
200 g/7 oz. Dolcelatte or other
  good melting blue cheese
crusty bread, to serve

DRESSING
3 tablespoons freshly squeezed
  orange juice
2 teaspoons sherry vinegar
$\frac{1}{2}$ teaspoon caster/granulated
  sugar
3 tablespoons extra virgin olive oil
1 tablespoon walnut oil
salt and freshly ground
  black pepper

SERVES 4-6

A lovely warm salad full of autumn[ ]
and flavours. Dolcelatte, meaning[ ]
is an Italian cow's milk blue chee[ ]
mild flavour and soft, creamy text[ ] is
a vegetarian cheese made without anim[ ] rennet
and is often described as a milder version of
Gorgonzola. It is perfect for this recipe, but
you could use other mild blue cheeses such
as Cambozola or a young Gorgonzola.

Preheat the oven to 200°C/fan 180°C/400°F/Gas 6 and line a large roasting pan with baking paper.

Cut the sweet potatoes into 2-cm/$\frac{3}{4}$-in. chunks and place in the prepared pan with the onion wedges. Add the oil and some salt and pepper, then stir well to make sure the chunks of sweet potato are evenly coated. Roast in the preheated oven for 40–50 minutes until the potatoes are caramelized and the onion browned. Remove from the oven and cool until just warm.

Meanwhile, place the pecans in a heavy non-stick frying pan/skillet and put on a medium heat. Add the maple syrup, paprika, cayenne pepper and salt. Heat gently until it starts to bubble, then cook for about 3 minutes until golden and sticky. Transfer the pecans to a piece of baking paper and let cool. Separate them if stuck together and chop roughly.

Cook the green beans in a saucepan of lightly salted, boiling water for 2 minutes. Drain and refresh under cold water. Drain well and pat dry.

To make the dressing, whisk together all the ingredients in a small bowl and season to taste. Put the spinach leaves in a large bowl and add the roasted sweet potato mixture, caramelized pecans and beans.

Heat the raclette machine or a conventional grill/broiler to the highest setting. Divide the cheese between the individual raclette trays and cook for 2–3 minutes until softened and bubbling. Dress the salad and divide between plates. Pour or scrape the cheese over the salad and serve with crusty bread.

GOAT'S CHEESE BRUSCHETTA

WITH ROASTED BEETROOT

500 g/1 lb. 2 oz. baby
   beetroot/beets
1 tablespoon olive oil
50 g/2 oz. walnuts, toasted
   and roughly chopped
4 slices of ciabatta
1 garlic clove, peeled but left
   whole
a handful each of rocket/
   arugula or mixed salad leaves
200 g/7 oz. Rocamadour or
   a goat's cheese log, sliced
salt and freshly ground
   black pepper
walnut or extra virgin olive oil
   and reduced balsamic vinegar
   (see note below), to serve

SERVES 4

Rounds of creamy white goat's cheese are melted under the raclette grill and served on a bruschetta with roasted baby beetroot/beets, salad leaves and toasted walnuts – a classic combination of flavours. If you can, serve the finished dish drizzled with a good-quality walnut oil. I like to use small individual rounds of goat's cheese known as Rocamadour, a well-known cheese from the department of Lot in south-west France (it is named after a local village). If you aren't able to find Rocamadour, use a log of goat's cheese, cut into 1-cm/½-in. thick slices.

Preheat the oven to 180°C/fan 160°C/350°F/Gas 4 and line a small roasting pan with baking paper.

Wash and dry the beetroot/beets (reserving any small tender leaves for the salad) and place in the prepared pan. Drizzle with the olive oil and season with salt and pepper. Cover the pan with foil and bake in the preheated oven for 40–45 minutes (depending on size) until tender. Once cooked, transfer to a bowl, cover with the foil and set aside to cool. Cut into halves or slices, discarding the skin.

Chargrill the ciabatta and rub all over with garlic. Place a slice of ciabatta on each serving plate and top with the beetroot/beets, walnuts, rocket/arugula leaves, walnut or olive oil, reduced balsamic vinegar and some salt and pepper.

Just before serving, heat the raclette machine or a conventional grill/broiler to its highest setting. Divide the cheese slices between the raclette trays and cook for 2–3 minutes until completely melted. As soon as the cheese is ready, slide it over the bruschetta and serve.

Note To make your own reduced balsamic vinegar, simply boil a 750-ml/3-cup bottle of inexpensive balsamic vinegar in a small saucepan for 6–8 minutes until it is reduced and syrup-like. Cool and store in a sterilized bottle. It will keep until used up.

RACLETTE OVER ROASTED POTATOES,

GARLIC & SHALLOTS WITH ROSEMARY

8 garlic cloves, unpeeled
8 small shallots, unpeeled
4 bay leaves, lightly bashed
2 sprigs of fresh rosemary,
   lightly bashed
1 kg/2 lb. 4 oz. unpeeled chat
   potatoes, or similar floury
   baby potatoes
4 tablespoons olive oil
200 g/7 oz. Raclette, cut into slices
salt and freshly ground
   black pepper
caperberries, silverskin/cocktail
   onions and a green salad,
   to serve

SERVES 6

This is my version of the classic raclette dish traditionally served with boiled new potatoes, cornichons and pickled onions (see page 83). Here the potatoes are roasted alongside shallots and garlic flavoured with rosemary and bay leaves. Once the vegetables are al dente they are 'smashed', drizzled with more olive oil and roasted again until they have a crispy, golden crust. At this stage they can now be transferred to the table for diners to help themselves and then the melted Raclette is spooned over. Serve them alongside a steak or slow-roasted lamb for a memorable dining experience.

Preheat the oven to 200°C/fan 180°C/400°F/Gas 6 and line a roasting pan with baking paper.

Put the garlic cloves, shallots and herbs into a saucepan and cover with cold water. Bring to the boil and simmer for 1 minute. Immediately drain and refresh the vegetables under cold running water. Pat dry and then peel the garlic and shallots, leaving them whole.

Place the potatoes, garlic, shallots, herbs, half the oil and some salt and pepper in the prepared roasting pan and stir so that everything is evenly coated in oil. Cover with foil and cook in the preheated oven for 30 minutes, checking they are al dente. Remove the pan from the oven, discarding the foil and herbs. Using a potato masher, 'smash' the potato mixture so it is roughly mashed. Drizzle over the remaining oil and return to the oven. Roast uncovered for a further 10–15 minutes until crisp and golden.

About 5 minutes before the potatoes are ready, heat the raclette machine or conventional grill/broiler to the highest setting. Place the tray of potatoes on the table for everyone to help themselves. Grill/broil the cheese slices either for 2 minutes or until bubbling and completely melted. Using a wooden spatula, scrape the cheese onto your plate of roasted potatoes and serve with capeberries, silverskin/cocktail onions and a green salad.

CAL-MEX BAKED GARLIC

WITH MELTED CHEESE

3 heads garlic
3 sprigs of fresh thyme
2 tablespoons extra virgin olive oil
6 slices of focaccia or sourdough
300 g/10½ oz. smoked Raclette
  or other smoked cheese, sliced

JALAPEÑO SALSA

2 tablespoons freshly chopped
  coriander/cilantro
1 garlic clove, crushed
3 fresh jalapeño peppers,
  finely chopped
1 spring onion/scallion,
  finely chopped
2 tablespoons freshly squeezed
  lime juice
salt and freshly ground
  black pepper

SERVES 6

I have very fond memories of the origin of this recipe. Travelling down the Californian coast with a girlfriend back in the day, we stopped for the night in Capitola, a small seaside town an hour or so south of San Fran. After a delicious coffee at the famous Mr Toots Coffeehouse (still there 25 years later), we dined in a cafe opposite (sorry, the name escapes me) and discovered for the very first time slow-roasted garlic, cooked as a whole bulb. It was simply served, with a chunk of just-ripe Camembert and griddled sourdough. It was sublime. Here it is all those years later, albeit with a wonderful smoked Raclette (smoked mozzarella or any good-quality smoked cheese can be substituted). It makes a great sharing appetizer dish, each person enjoying half a garlic bulb.

Preheat the oven to 200°C/fan 180°C/400°F/Gas 6.

Carefully cut the tops from the garlic bulbs, reserving them and sit each bulb on a piece of foil about 20-cm/8-in. square. Add a little thyme, salt and pepper to each one and then drizzle with oil. Pop the garlic tops back in place and wrap each one up into a small parcel, sealing the foil. Cook in the preheated oven for about 45 minutes until the garlic is completely softened.

Meanwhile, make the salsa. Place all the ingredients in a bowl and stir to combine. Season to taste with salt and pepper.

When ready to serve, griddle the focaccia or sourdough and drizzle each one with oil. Heat the raclette machine or conventional grill/broiler to its highest setting and divide the Raclette slices between the raclette trays. Grill/broil the cheese slices for 2 minutes or until the cheese is bubbling and completely melted. Place a slice of griddled bread on each serving plate and spread with the softened paste from the roasted garlic bulbs. Scrape or slide the melted cheese over the bread and serve topped with the salsa.

TALEGGIO & ROASTED VEGETABLE WRAPS

WITH TOMATO & ONION JAM

1 medium aubergine/eggplant/
  trimmed
2 small red (bell) peppers,
  quartered and deseeded
2 medium courgettes/zucchini,
  trimmed
4 tablespoons olive oil
6 x 22-cm/8$\frac{1}{2}$-in. tortilla wraps
a handful of mixed salad leaves
  per person
250 g/9 oz. Taleggio, sliced
3 tablespoons chopped preserved
  lemons
salt and freshly ground
  black pepper
dukkah and lemon wedges,
  to serve

TOMATO & ONION JAM
75 g/$\frac{2}{3}$ cup sun-dried tomatoes
  in oil, drained and chopped
1 onion, finely chopped
2 garlic cloves, chopped
2 red chillies/chiles, sliced
25 g/2$\frac{1}{2}$ tablespoons raisins
125 g/$\frac{2}{3}$ cup minus 2 teaspoons
  caster/granulated sugar
80 ml/5$\frac{1}{2}$ tablespoons red wine
  vinegar
1 teaspoon salt

SERVES 6

Just reading the title of this recipe transports me to the southern Mediterranean, perhaps Naples or Sicily – oh, that sounds good! Taleggio – an Italian cheese made from cow's milk – is a seamless blend of creaminess and acidity. The edible, orangey-red smeared rind is made by using five different cheese moulds, giving the cheese its renowned look and flavour. Fontina is a good substitute, and at a pinch you could use Brie or Camembert.

First make the tomato and onion jam. Place all the ingredients in a saucepan with enough water to just cover everything and heat gently, stirring, until it reaches the boil. Simmer uncovered over a low heat, for 30 minutes until thickened, stirring from time to time so that the jam does not catch on the base of the pan. Immediately transfer to a sterilized jar. Seal with a vinegar-safe lid and set aside to cool.

Preheat the oven to 180°C/fan 160°C/350°F/Gas 4.

Heat a griddle pan until hot. Cut the aubergine/eggplant, (bell) peppers and courgettes/zucchini into slices, all roughly the same size. Place them all together in a bowl and add the oil, salt and pepper. Toss together until they are evenly coated. Cook the vegetables in batches on the griddle until evenly charred and just softened. Wrap loosely in foil and keep warm.

Loosely wrap the tortillas in a large sheet of foil and place in the oven for 5 minutes to soften and warm through.

Heat the raclette machine or conventional grill/broiler to the highest setting. Pop the cheese slices on the raclette trays and scatter over the preserved lemon. Cook under the heat for 3–4 minutes until the cheese starts to run.

Place a warm tortilla wrap on each serving plate, then divide the roasted vegetables between them. Slide or scrape over the melted cheese, add some tomato and onion jam, sprinkle with dukkah, wrap and eat.

TEX-MEX GRILLED CORN

WITH SMOKED RACLETTE

6 ears of corn
1 tablespoon olive oil
50 g/¼ cup mayonnaise
 (see page 145)
50 g/¼ cup sour cream
1 small garlic clove, crushed
a pinch of cayenne pepper
12 slices smoked Raclette
 (300–350 g/10½–12½ oz.),
 or a similar smoked cheese
2 tablespoons freshly chopped
 coriander/cilantro
3 tablespoons freshly grated
 Parmesan
salt and freshly ground
 black pepper
lime wedges, to serve

SERVES 6

Based on a classic Mexican corn dish called elote, sweetcorn cobs are grilled over hot coals or a barbecue and slathered with mayonnaise, chilli/chili powder and freshly squeezed lime juice. Mexican cheese called cotija, similar to a mild feta when young, but more like Parmesan when it is aged (as used here), is then grated over the top and finally fresh coriander/cilantro is scattered over. It is so yummy, if a little messy, and perfect as a raclette recipe. Prepare the corn and then serve it topped with slices of melted smoked cheese. If you are able to find smoked Raclette use that; if not, any good-quality smoked cheese will work.

Blanch the corn cobs in a pan of lightly salted boiling water for 5 minutes (if the husks are still attached, pull them back and remove any silky threads). Drain and immediately refresh under cold water. Dry thoroughly. Rub the corn cobs with oil and season with salt and pepper. Griddle them on a preheated grill pan/griddle until charred on all sides.

Meanwhile, blend the mayonnaise, sour cream, garlic, cayenne and a little salt and pepper together in a bowl.

Heat the raclette machine or a conventional grill/broiler to the highest setting. Place the Raclette slices on the raclette trays and cook for 3–4 minutes until bubbling and completely melted.

Arrange the corn cobs on a platter for diners to help themselves. Spread a little of the mayonnaise mixture on the corn and scatter over the Parmesan. As soon as the cheese is ready, scrape or slide it onto the corn, add a little extra cayenne and the coriander/cilantro and serve with lime juice squeezed over.

GOAT'S CHEESE ROUNDS

WITH HONEY, THYME & GRAPES

6 slices smoked bacon (optional)
200 g/7 oz. goat's cheese log
1–2 tablespoons clear honey
2 teaspoons picked thyme leaves
1 teaspoon fennel seeds,
  roughly ground
1 tablespoon sesame seeds
1 tablespoon walnut oil
freshly ground black pepper
grapes, ripe pears and walnut
  bread, to serve

SERVES 6

Sweet and savoury combine here as an appetizer, rather than a dessert, as the sharpness of the cheese is just enough for the honey to sweeten slightly but not overpower, therefore providing the perfect balance in a super simple dish.

Dry fry the bacon slices, if using, in a frying pan/skillet over a high heat until crisped to your liking.

Heat the raclette machine or conventional grill/broiler to the highest setting. Cut the cheese log into 6 x 1-cm/$\frac{1}{2}$ -in. slices and place each slice on a raclette tray. Top each with a little honey, thyme, ground fennel and sesame seeds. Season with pepper and drizzle with a little walnut oil.

Place the goat's cheese under the grill/broiler and cook for 5–6 minutes until it is melted and bubbling. At the same time, reheat the bacon slices on the hot plate of the raclette machine (or in the frying pan/skillet) for 2–3 minutes.

Scrape the cooked cheese onto plates and serve with the bacon, slices of walnut bread, some sweet grapes and nicely ripe pears.

BRÛLÉED SUMMER BERRIES

WITH FETA

400 g/14 oz. prepared fresh
  summer berries, such as
  strawberries, raspberries,
  blueberries etc
150 g/5½ oz. mascarpone
150 g/5½ oz. feta, drained and
  crumbled
150 g/⅔ cup crème fraîche
2 tablespoons maple syrup
½ teaspoon vanilla extract
2 tablespoons demerara/raw
  brown sugar
¼ teaspoon ground cinnamon
langues de chat biscuits/cookies,
  to serve

SERVES 6–8

Some of our favourite food combinations balance the sweet with the savoury – cheese and honey, meat with dried fruits, a cheese platter with fresh figs. Although a traditional raclette dish is a savoury one, there is no reason why you shouldn't serve it as a dessert, as here. Feta, blended with mascarpone, crème fraîche and maple syrup, forms a creamy blanket over mixed summer berries topped with a scattering of brown sugar and cinnamon. They are then lightly grilled/broiled until the feta cream oozes and warms the fruits beneath a crunchy topping. You can either use traditional raclette dishes or individual gratin dishes.

Divide the prepared berries between 8 raclette dishes or shallow ramekins and set aside.

In a food processor, blend together the mascarpone, feta, crème fraîche, maple syrup and vanilla extract until as smooth as possible. Divide the mixture between the fruit dishes and carefully spread over the top. Scatter with the demerara sugar and a little cinnamon.

Heat the raclette machine or grill/broiler to the highest setting. Pop the dishes under the heat and cook for about 5–6 minutes until the tops are brûléed and bubbling. Cool very briefly before serving with langues de chat biscuits.

PEACHES WITH RACLETTE & CINNAMON

50 g/3½ tablespoons unsalted butter
50 g/¼ cup soft brown sugar
½ teaspoon ground cinnamon
4 fresh peaches, halved and stoned
100 ml/7 tablespoons Pedro Ximénez, Madeira or Marsala
50 ml/3½ tablespoons double/heavy cream, plus extra to serve
4 thick slices brioche loaf
4 slices raclette cheese, or 100 g/3½ oz. raclette, thinly sliced
2 tablespoons flaked/slivered almonds, toasted

SERVES 4

If you find yourself with fresh peaches that are still a little under ripe, rather than setting them in the sunshine to ripen further, why not give this recipe a try. Pedro Ximénez is a divine sweet sherry from Jerez in Spain's sherry-producing region. It is raisin-y, with a somewhat chocolatey flavour that blends beautifully with both the peaches and the melted Raclette. You could substitute either Madeira or Marsala for the sherry, although Pedro Ximénez is best.

Heat the butter, sugar and cinnamon together in a heavy frying pan/skillet. When bubbling, add the peach halves, cut side down and cook over a high heat for 2–3 minutes until lightly golden. Remove the peaches with a slotted spoon to a foil-lined tray. Return the frying pan/skillet to the heat and stir in the Pedro Ximénez and cream. Simmer for 5 minutes until you have a thickened, caramel sauce. Keep warm.

Heat the raclette machine to its highest setting so the top plate is hot. Place the pan of peaches on the heat to keep warm.

Meanwhile, toast the brioche slices either under the raclette grill or a conventional grill/broiler and arrange on warm serving plates.

Lay the Raclette slices on the individual raclette trays and grill/broil for 3–4 minutes until bubbling and melted. Carefully spoon 2 peach halves onto each slice of brioche and slide the melted cheese over the top. Immediately drizzle with the warm caramel sauce, a little more cream and serve scattered with the toasted almonds.

OIL
FONDUE

SOUTHERN CHICKEN BURGERS

WITH CABBAGE & LIME SLAW

2 chicken breast fillets
125 ml/$\frac{1}{2}$ cup buttermilk
4 brioche burger rolls
a handful of salad leaves
    per guest
sunflower oil for deep-frying
mayonnaise (see page 145),
    to serve

CABBAGE, FENNEL & LIME SLAW
125 g/4$\frac{1}{2}$ oz. red cabbage,
    shredded
$\frac{1}{2}$ fennel, shredded
$\frac{1}{2}$ onion, thinly sliced
2 teaspoons freshly squeezed
    lime juice
1$\frac{1}{2}$ teaspoons caster/
    granulated sugar
1 teaspoon sea salt

BREADCRUMB COATING
100 g/1$\frac{1}{4}$ cups dried
    breadcrumbs
1 teaspoon mustard powder
$\frac{1}{2}$ teaspoon sea salt
$\frac{1}{2}$ teaspoon smoked paprika
$\frac{1}{4}$ teaspoon freshly ground
    black pepper

SERVES 4

This is my fondue version of fried chicken burgers. Strips of chicken are marinated overnight in buttermilk, which helps to tenderize the meat. Coated in breadcrumbs, the chicken pieces can then be skewered with fondue forks and deep-fried at the table. Diners make their own little burgers with brioche rolls, lettuce leaves and the delicious and tangy fennel and lime slaw.

Cut the chicken breast fillets into 2–3-cm/$\frac{3}{4}$–1$\frac{1}{4}$-in. pieces and place in a shallow dish. Pour over the buttermilk, cover and chill overnight. This will tenderize the chicken. The next day, remove the chicken from the fridge and return to room temperature for 30 minutes.

To make the slaw, place the cabbage, fennel and onion in a bowl. Combine the lime juice, sugar and salt and stir well, then add to the slaw, stirring to combine. Set aside until required.

Combine all the breadcrumb coating ingredients in a bowl. Remove the chicken pieces from the buttermilk and immediately dip into the crumb mixture, pressing down well and making sure they are totally coated. Cover and place on the table with the brioche rolls, the chicken pieces, bowls of the slaw, lettuce and some mayonnaise.

Heat enough oil to come no more than a third of the way up the sides of a metal fondue pan and heat on the stovetop until it reaches 180°C/350°F. As soon as the oil reaches temperature, very carefully transfer the pot to the tabletop burner. Diners can now skewer the chicken pieces and gently lower into the hot oil, letting them cook for 2–3 minutes until golden and cooked through. Allow to cool for a minute or two. Assemble the rolls and as soon as the chicken has cooled a little, top with the bun lids and eat.

CHICKEN & DUCK FONDUE

WITH TUNISIAN RELISH

500 g/1 lb. 2 oz. skinless, boneless
  chicken breasts or thighs
500 g/1 lb. 2 oz. duck breast, with
  the fat trimmed and reserved
750 ml–1.25 litres/3¼–5 cups
  peanut or safflower oil
couscous tossed with
  pomegranate seeds, pistachio
  nuts and coriander/cilantro and
  steamed carrots, to serve

TUNISIAN RELISH
4 large tomatoes, skinned
  and deseeded
peel of 1 preserved lemon
2 tablespoons harissa or tomato
  purée/paste
a large handful of fresh coriander/
  cilantro, chopped
2 tablespoons olive oil
sea salt

SERVES 6

Fondues don't have to be Swiss – they are also a fabulously easy way to throw a North African-themed dinner party. Serve platters of couscous tossed with herbs and sautéed vegetables, pass around bowls of relish, then have your guests cook their own chicken and duck skewers. The rendered duck fat added to the cooking oil gives a wonderful depth of flavour.

To make the Tunisian relish, chop the tomatoes and preserved lemon peel very finely and put into a bowl. Stir in the harissa or tomato purée/paste, coriander/cilantro and olive oil. Season with salt and set aside for a few hours to allow the flavours to develop.

Cut the chicken and duck into 1-cm/½-in. strips and thread strips of each onto the skewers, about 50 g/1¾ oz. per skewer, leaving about 4 cm/1½ in. clear at the end, so the skewer can rest it on the bottom of the pot without sticking. Arrange on a serving platter. Set platters of couscous and bowls of relish on the table.

Fill a metal fondue pot one-third full with oil and add the duck fat trimmings. Heat the oil to 180°C/350°F or until a cube of bread browns in 40 seconds. Very carefully transfer the pot to its tabletop burner. Remove the duck fat when it becomes brown.

Invite guests to cook the skewers of duck and chicken in the hot oil for 2 minutes or until cooked through, then eat with the couscous and relish.

BURMESE-STYLE SPICED PORK

WITH SWEET GARLIC SAUCE

500 g/1 lb. 2 oz. pork fillet,
    very thinly sliced (see page 115)
2 teaspoons ground turmeric
1/4 teaspoon salt
3 tablespoons fish sauce
sunflower oil, for deep-frying
boiled rice, fresh herbs and lime
    wedges, to serve

SWEET GARLIC SAUCE
2 large garlic cloves
4 red chillies/chiles, chopped
1 tablespoon peanut or
    sunflower oil
60 ml/4 tablespoons tamarind
    paste
60 g/4 tablespoons palm sugar,
    grated
2–3 tablespoons soy sauce

SERVES 4

Street food in Myanmar (previously known as Burma), as with all Far-East Asian cities, is where you really get a taste for a country's cuisine; real food for real people. The buzz that comes with trawling through the streets, markets or beachside stalls is maybe part of the reason, as is the feeling of food being shared, ad hoc, on the move. This recipe is typical of the type of dishes regularly cooked by street-food vendors in Myanmar. Serve with rice and lots of lovely fresh Asian herbs – basil, coriander/cilantro and mint and a good squeeze of lime juice.

Place the sliced pork in a bowl and add the turmeric and salt. Rub gently to lightly coat the meat then stir in the fish sauce. Cover and refrigerate for at least 4 hours.

Remove from the fridge 30 minutes before cooking to return to room temperature. Divide the meat between 8 skewers, threading a few slices onto each one, arrange on a large platter and set aside until required.

To make the sauce, place the garlic and chillies/chiles in a pestle and mortar or a blender and pound or blend until you have a rough paste. Heat the oil in a small frying pan/skillet and gently fry the chilli paste for 2–3 minutes soft and fragrant. Add the tamarind paste, sugar, soy sauce and 50 ml water and simmer until the sauce is thick and glossy, about 5 minutes. Keep warm.

Place the pork, sweet garlic sauce, fresh herbs, lime wedges and some plain boiled rice in bowls on the table.

Pour enough oil into a metal fondue pan to come no more than a third of the way up the sides and heat on the stovetop until it reaches 180°C/350°F. As soon as the oil reaches its required temperature, very carefully transfer the pot to the tabletop burner. Diners can gently lower the pork skewers into the hot oil and cook for 1–2 minutes until crisp, golden and cooked through. Serve with all the accompaniments.

JAPANESE BEEF

WITH MISO HOLLANDAISE & JAPANESE PICKLES

60 ml/4 tablespoons soy sauce
60 ml/4 tablespoons sake
30 ml/2 tablespoons mirin
1½ tablespoons caster/
   granulated sugar
500 g/1 lb. 2 oz. beef fillet,
   very thinly sliced (see page 115)
cooked sticky rice, garnished with
   black sesame seeds, to serve

JAPANESE PICKLES
100 g/3½ oz. root ginger, peeled
   and very thinly sliced
200 g/7 oz. Chinese cabbage,
   shredded
150 ml/⅔ cup rice wine vinegar
75 g caster/granulated sugar
1 teaspoon sea salt

MISO HOLLANDAISE
95 g/6½ tablespoons unsalted
   butter
2 free-range egg yolks
1 tablespoon rice wine vinegar
1 teaspoon white or yellow
   miso paste

SERVES 4

I love the simple nature of many Japanese dishes, the harmony of flavours, colours and ingredients, the balance of sweet, salty and sharp. Here the salty soy and sweet mirin in the marinade combine well with the sharpness of the pickles, softened with the creaminess of the hollandaise enhanced by a salty hit of miso paste. The pickles can be made ahead of time as they keep well. Make the hollandaise just before frying the beef, it will keep warm for a little while. This is perfect as an appetizer or a light lunch.

For the pickles, bring a small pan of water to the boil, add the ginger and cook for 2 minutes, drain and cool a little. Squeeze out as much water as you can, pat dry and place in a jar. Place the cabbage in a bowl. Put the vinegar, sugar and salt in a pan with 100 ml/7 tablespoons water, bring to the boil, stirring so the sugar dissolves, then let cool for 30 minutes. Pour enough of the syrup over the sliced ginger to just cover it and pour the rest over the cabbage. Cover each one and set aside until cold.

Combine the soy sauce, sake, mirin and sugar in a small saucepan and heat gently, stirring until the sugar is dissolved. Set aside until completely cold. Add the beef to the pan and leave to marinate for 1 hour. Drain the beef and pat dry just before cooking. Thread the meat onto 8 skewers.

Make the hollandaise. Place the butter in a small pan and melt over a low heat without stirring. Then bring to the boil and cook for several minutes until it turns a nutty brown. Blend the egg yolks, vinegar and miso together in a bowl until smooth. Very gradually whisk in the brown butter until the sauce is thickened and all the butter incorporated.

Place small bowls of cooked sticky rice, the pickles and the hollandaise sauce on the table along with a platter of the beef.

Pour enough oil into a metal fondue pot to come no more than a third of the way up the sides and heat on the stovetop until it reaches 180°C/350°F. As soon as the oil reaches its required temperature, transfer the pot very carefully to the tabletop burner. Diners can gently lower the beef skewers, 4 at a time, in the hot oil for 30–60 seconds until cooked through. Serve with the rice, pickles and hollandaise sauce.

FONDUE
BOURGUIGNONNE

1.25 kg/2¾ lb. beef fillet, finely sliced
750 ml–1.25 litres/3¼–5 cups peanut
   or safflower oil
sea salt and freshly ground
   black pepper
salad leaves and crusty bread,
   to serve

MAYONNAISE DIPS
1 egg and 2 egg yolks, at room
   temperature
2 teaspoons Dijon mustard
2 teaspoons freshly squeezed lemon
   juice
350 ml/1½ cups sunflower
   or safflower oil
salt
½ teaspoon curry powder
1 teaspoon hot mustard
1 tablespoon tomato ketchup
1 teaspoon horseradish sauce

SKORDALIA
250 g/9 oz. floury potatoes
   (about 2 medium)
300 g/10½ oz. celeriac/celery root,
   about 240 g/8½ oz. after peeling
2–3 garlic cloves, crushed
½ teaspoon salt
1 egg yolk
125 ml/½ cup extra virgin olive oil
freshly squeezed juice of ½ lemon

GREEN SALSA
2 limes
4 spring onions/scallions, finely sliced
2 garlic cloves, crushed
1 small bunch of flat-leaf parsley,
   about 15 g/½ oz., finely chopped
a large bunch of sorrel, about
   30 g/1 oz., finely chopped (if
   unavailable, use rocket/arugula)
2 tablespoons olive oil

SERVES 6

The meat for this dish should be very thinly sliced – to make this easier, freeze the whole piece of beef for 2–3 hours before slicing. Traditionally, this fondue is served with several mayonnaise-based sauces flavoured with curry powder, mustard, tomato sauce or horseradish, but do try the deliciously different accompaniments suggested here – skordalia, a garlicky sauce from Greece, and green salsa, made with lemony sorrel leaves.

For the mayonnaise, put the whole egg and yolks into a food processor. Add the mustard, a pinch of salt and 1 teaspoon lemon juice. Blend until smooth, then gradually pour in the oil until the mixture is thick and creamy. Blend in another teaspoon of lemon juice, and 1–2 teaspoons warm water if the mixture is too thick. Divide between 4 small bowls and stir curry powder into one, mustard into another, tomato ketchup into the third and horseradish into the fourth.

For the skordalia, cut the potatoes and celeriac/celery root into even chunks. Place in a saucepan, cover with water, bring to the boil, cover and simmer until tender. Drain, return to the pan and cover with a kitchen towel to dry out for 5 minutes. Mash until smooth, then beat in the garlic, salt and egg yolk. Gradually beat in the oil, then the lemon juice. If the mixture is too thick, add a little warm water.

For the green salsa, grate the zest of the limes into a small food processor or large mortar. Add the spring onions/scallions, garlic and parsley and work to a coarse mixture. Add the juice of 1 lime, then the sorrel and oil to form a coarse green paste. Season with salt and pepper.

Dry the sliced beef well with kitchen paper, then arrange on a serving platter. Fill a metal fondue pot one-third full with oil. Heat the oil to 190°C/375°F or until a cube of bread browns in 30 seconds. Very carefully transfer the pot to its tabletop burner. Spear or thread a piece of beef onto a skewer and lower it into the hot oil for about 30–60 seconds (if you thread the meat a little way up the skewer, the skewer can rest on the bottom of the pot without the meat sticking). Serve with the dips, skordalia, green salsa, salad and bread.

LAMB FONDUE
WITH TOASTED BAHARAT

1.25 kg/2¾ lb. lamb fillet,
    thinly sliced
750 ml–1.25 litres/3¼–5 cups
    peanut or safflower oil
flatbreads, hummus, salad leaves
    and plain yogurt, to serve
    (optional)

BAHARAT SPICE MIX
125 g/1 cup blanched almonds
125 g/1 cup shelled pistachios
4 tablespoons sesame seeds
1 tablespoon black peppercorns
1½ tablespoons cumin seeds
1 tablespoon coriander seeds
2 cinnamon sticks, crumbled
1–2 tablespoons sweet paprika
½ teaspoon grated nutmeg

SERVES 6

Lamb makes a great variation on the classic beef fondue. To make the lamb easier to slice, freeze it for about 1 hour first. Baharat is a fragrant Middle Eastern spice mix – it can be a combination of many herbs, spices and flowers, and here nuts have been added to soften the blend.

To make the baharat, put the almonds and pistachios into a dry frying pan/skillet and toast for a few minutes until brown. Let cool, then transfer to a food processor and grind coarsely. Toast the sesame seeds in the pan, then add to the processor and pulse briefly. Put the black peppercorns, cumin, coriander and crumbled cinnamon into the pan and dry-toast for a few minutes until fragrant. Transfer to a spice grinder, add the paprika and nutmeg and grind to a powder. Alternatively, use a mortar and pestle. Transfer to a sterilized jar, add the nut and seed mixture and shake well. The mixture will keep for 1 month, and can be used to flavour meats or vegetables, or as a dip with bread and oil.

To prepare the fondue, pat the lamb dry with kitchen paper and arrange on a serving platter. Spoon the baharat into 6 small bowls.

Fill a metal fondue pot one-third full with oil. Heat the oil on the stovetop until it reaches 190°C/375°F or until a cube of bread browns in 30 seconds. Very carefully transfer the pot to its tabletop burner. Invite each guest to thread a piece of lamb onto a skewer and dip into the hot oil for 15–30 seconds. Dip the hot lamb into the baharat, then eat. Alternatively, make flatbread wraps with the lamb, hummus, salad and yogurt.

CRISPY VEGETABLE FONDUE

WITH CITRUS DIPPING SAUCE

2 sweet potatoes
1 small red (bell) pepper
1 small yellow (bell) pepper
1 small head of broccoli,
    divided into 12 pieces
4 courgettes/zucchini, cut
    diagonally into 1.5-cm/
    ½-in. slices
12 mushrooms, halved
2 eggs, separated
1 tablespoon olive oil
125 g/1 cup minus 1 tablespoon
    plain/all-purpose flour
a pinch of salt
750 ml–1.25 litres/3¼–5 cups
    peanut or safflower oil

CITRUS DIPPING SAUCE
125 ml/½ cup freshly squeezed
    lime or lemon juice
1 tablespoon runny honey
1 tablespoon wholegrain mustard
1 tablespoon fish sauce
sea salt and freshly ground
    black pepper

SERVES 6

Fritto misto and tempura are fantastic ways to serve vegetables, but since they are best straight from the pan, they can be a bit of a hassle to cook and serve. Often the cook gets stuck in the kitchen while other people enjoy themselves. Served as a fondue, it becomes a happy, communal task, and the taste couldn't get any fresher.

To prepare the sweet potatoes, cut into 1.5-cm/½-in. slices, then cut these into quarters. Put into a saucepan, add cold water to cover, bring to the boil, then drain and cool under cold water. Dry well.

Cut each pepper lengthways into 12 and discard the seeds. Prepare all the other vegetables, pat dry with kitchen paper and arrange on serving platters.

Put all the dipping sauce ingredients into a bowl and mix well. Divide between 6 dipping bowls.

Put the egg yolks, olive oil and 200 ml/¾ cup iced water into a bowl and whisk well. Whisk in the salt and flour to form a smooth batter; do not overmix. Whisk the egg whites in a second bowl, until stiff but not dry. Fold into the batter.

Fill a metal fondue pot no more than one-third full with oil. Heat the oil on the stovetop until it reaches 200°C/400°F, or until a piece of bread turns golden in 25 seconds.

Transfer the pot of hot oil very carefully to its tabletop burner to keep hot (make sure the temperature doesn't drop or the vegetables will be greasy). Invite guests to spear the pieces of vegetable onto fondue forks, dip into the batter, then fry for 2–3 minutes, until golden and crispy. Serve with the citrus dipping sauce.

CRISPY 5-SPICE TOFU

WITH SWEET & SOUR CHILLI SAUCE

500 g/1 lb. 2 oz. firm tofu, drained
40 g/4¾ tablespoons self-raising/
   rising flour
1 teaspoon Chinese 5-spice
   powder
½ teaspoon sea salt
a pinch of cayenne pepper
2 carrots, shredded
1 cucumber, deseeded and
   shredded
50 g/2 oz. bean sprouts, trimmed
4 spring onions/scallions,
   shredded
a few sprigs each of Thai basil,
   mint and coriander/cilantro
sunflower oil, for deep-frying
jasmine rice, to serve

CHILLI SAUCE
6 large red chillies/chiles
4 garlic cloves, roughly chopped
2 teaspoons grated root ginger
2 teaspoons fish sauce
100 ml/⅓ cup plus 1 tablespoon
   rice wine vinegar
100 g/½ cup granulated sugar

SERVES 6

I love deep-fried tofu; the crispy outside houses a soft and tender centre that is ideally suited to absorb the aromatics of Chinese 5-spice powder. I tend to make large quantities of the chilli/chili sauce as it keeps well in the fridge and is great with all types of foods like burgers, sandwiches or simple grilled fish and chicken. Firm tofu is best for this dish as it is robust enough to both coat in the spice mix and hold its shape on the fondue skewers.

To make the sauce, put the chillies/chiles, garlic and ginger in a food processor and blitz until fairly smooth, then transfer to a saucepan with the fish sauce, vinegar and the sugar. Bring to the boil and simmer gently for 10 minutes or until thickened with a jam-like consistency. Spoon directly into a sterilized jar, seal with a vinegar-safe lid and set aside until required.

Cut the tofu into 2-cm/¾-in. cubes. Sift the flour into a bowl and stir in the Chinese 5-spice, sea salt and cayenne pepper until evenly combined. Toss the tofu pieces in the spiced flour mixture until evenly coated. Arrange on a platter and place on the table.

Place small bowls of the chilli/chili sauce, shredded vegetables, bean sprouts, spring onions/scallions and herbs on the table.

Pour enough oil into a metal fondue pot to come no more than a third of the way up the sides and heat on the stovetop until it reaches 180°C/350°F. As soon as the oil reaches temperature, very carefully transfer the pot to the tabletop burner. Diners can now skewer the tofu, lower into the hot oil and cook for about 2 minutes until crisp and golden. Serve with bowls of jasmine rice topped with the tofu, chilli/chili sauce and all the remaining accompaniments.

POLENTA FRIES

WITH MAYONNAISE & CHIMICHURRI

1½ teaspoons salt
75 g/½ cup instant polenta/
  cornmeal, plus 4 tablespoons
  extra for crumb coating
30 g/2 tablespoons butter
30 g/½ cup freshly grated
  Parmesan
freshly ground black pepper
sunflower oil, for deep-frying
mayonnaise (see page 145),
  to serve

CHIMICHURRI SAUCE
15 g/½ oz. fresh coriander/
  cilantro
15 g/½ oz. fresh parsley
1 teaspoon dried oregano
2 garlic cloves, chopped
½ teaspoon smoked paprika
150 ml/⅔ cup extra virgin
  olive oil
1 tablespoon red wine vinegar
a pinch of caster/granulated
  sugar

SERVES 6–8

These little polenta/cornmeal cubes, crispy on the outside, soft and creamy on the inside make a great appetizer served with the tangy herb dip. The polenta is best made ahead of time so it can set firmly before being cubed and dipped into extra polenta crumbs. Served with a glass of crisp, dry white wine.

To make the polenta, line a 20-cm/8-in. square baking pan with baking paper. Bring 500 ml/2 cups water to the boil in a heavy-based saucepan, add the salt and then stir in the polenta/cornmeal. Cook over a medium heat, stirring with a wooden spoon for 4–5 minutes or until the polenta is paste-like and comes away from the sides of the pan.

Remove from the heat and immediately stir in the butter, Parmesan and some black pepper. Pour the paste into the prepared pan, spread flat and set aside until completely cold. Turn the polenta out onto a board and cut into 2-cm/¾-in. cubes. Put the 4 tablespoons of polenta in a shallow bowl and add the cubes. Turn to coat thoroughly and arrange on a larger platter.

To make the chimichurri sauce, place all the ingredients in a food processor and blend until fairly smooth. Season to taste and spoon into a bowl. Place on the table along with the platter of polenta cubes and bowls of mayonnaise.

Heat enough oil to come no more than a third of the way up the sides of a metal fondue pan and heat on the stovetop until it reaches 180°C/350°F. As soon as the oil reaches temperature, very carefully transfer the pot to the tabletop burner. Diners can now skewer the polenta cubes and cook, in batches, in the hot oil for about 2–3 minutes until golden and heated through. Serve with the chimichurri and mayonnaise.

BAGNA CAUDA

200 ml/¾ cup extra virgin olive oil
4–5 garlic cloves, crushed
12 anchovy fillets, mashed,
 about 50–75 g/2–2½ oz.
60 g/4 tablespoons walnut
 paste or almond butter,
 or 2 tablespoons each of
 walnut oil and butter

TO SERVE
a selection of vegetables, trimmed
 and cut into bite-sized pieces
crusty bread or breadsticks
 (optional)

SERVES 4–6 AS AN APPETIZER

Bagna cauda is a rich garlic and anchovy dip from Piedmont in the north of Italy. It isn't strictly a fondue, but is traditionally served hot from a small fondue dish. Serve with a selection of vegetables, including chicory leaves, fennel, celery and cardoons (a relative of the artichoke). Other choices are (bell) peppers, carrots, mushrooms, cherry tomatoes, cauliflower and regular artichoke hearts. It's also marvellous just with bread, or the Walnut Grissini on page 29.

Put the oil, garlic and anchovies into a small saucepan and heat gently on the stovetop, taking care not to brown the garlic. Stir in the walnut paste or walnut oil and butter and cook for 2–3 minutes.

Transfer to a fondue pot and set over a tabletop burner to keep the mixture warm. Serve with the vegetables and bread, if using, for dipping.

Variation: Creamy Bagna Cauda

Put 400 ml/1⅔ cups single/light cream into a small saucepan and bring to the boil. Simmer until reduced by half – about 5 minutes. Put 1 tablespoon butter into a small fondue pot and melt over a low heat. Add 12 anchovy fillets, finely chopped, and 4 crushed garlic cloves and cook briefly, mashing together and taking care not to let the garlic brown. Stir in the reduced cream and transfer the bowl to its tabletop burner to keep warm. Serve with vegetables and bread.

SCALLOPS
WITH GARLIC & LEMON BUTTER

24 large scallops
50 g/¾ cup dried plain
   breadcrumbs
125 g/9 tablespoons butter
4 smoked garlic cloves, finely
   chopped
finely grated zest of 1 lemon
2 tablespoons freshly chopped
   parsley
50 g/⅔ cup freshly grated
   Parmesan
salt and freshly ground
   black pepper
sunflower oil, for deep-frying
lemon wedges and French bread,
   to serve

SERVES 4

Traditionally, in France, fresh scallops are served in their shells topped with a little cream, fresh breadcrumbs, butter, garlic and parsley and then grilled until the crumbs are crisp and golden and the scallops beneath cooked to perfection. Here the raw scallops are coated with breadcrumbs first, before being deep-fried in the fondue pot at the table. They are then served with a dip of melted garlic, lemon and parsley butter and a little grated Parmesan.

Wash and dry the scallops and remove the corals (freeze to use later in a stock). Season the breadcrumbs with a little salt and pepper and pop into a shallow bowl. Add the scallops and turn over a few times until they are completely coated and no flesh remains exposed. Place on a platter and set aside.

Melt the butter in a small pan, add the garlic and gently fry for 3–4 minutes until very soft, but not browned. Add the lemon zest, cook briefly, then stir in the parsley and season with pepper. Keep warm.

Place small bowls of Parmesan on the table with the scallops, garlic butter sauce, lemon wedges and some French bread.

Pour enough oil into your fondue pot to come no more than a third of the way up the sides and heat on the stovetop until it reaches 180°C/350°F. When the oil reaches temperature, very carefully transfer the pot to the tabletop burner. Skewer the scallops and cook in the hot oil for 1–2 minutes until the crumbs are crisp and golden. Serve the scallops dipped into the garlic butter sauce and sprinkled with Parmesan. Mop up any extra sauce and juices with the bread.

PRAWN & CALAMARI SKEWERS

WITH ALMOND & BASIL DIP

500 g/1 lb. 2 oz. small squid,
   about 16
500 g/1 lb. 2 oz. large prawns/
   jumbo shrimp
750 ml–1.25 litres/3¼–5 cups
   peanut or safflower oil
lemon and lime wedges, to serve

ALMOND & BASIL DIP
75 g/½ cup blanched almonds
finely grated zest of 2 lemons
   or 4 limes
a small bunch of basil, about
   15 g/½ oz.
a small bunch of flat-leaf parsley,
   about 15 g/½ oz.
1 tablespoon freshly squeezed
   lime juice
3 tablespoons extra virgin olive oil
sea salt flakes

SERVES 8 AS AN APPETIZER

A sizzling, very adaptable first course. Serve it with this almond and basil dip for a Mediterranean feast – or, if you substitute Thai basil and lime, you have the perfect appetizer for an Asian meal. The tentacles of the squid look most dramatic, but if they are unavailable, you can use just the bodies.

To make the almond and basil dip, put the almonds and lemon or lime zest into a food processor and grind coarsely. Add the remaining ingredients and grind again. Add salt to taste and set aside.

If the squid are whole, clean them by pulling the tentacles out of the body, then cut off the rosette of tentacles and press out the tiny hard piece in the middle. Pull the pen (the transparent wafer) out of the body and discard it. Remove the thin purplish skin if preferred. Rinse the bodies, pat dry and cut in half. Using a sharp knife, lightly score the inside surface of the bodies with criss-cross hatching. Dry well with paper towels.

Peel and devein the prawns/shrimp (see page 145), leaving the tails attached. Thread a prawn or a piece of squid onto each long skewer. Arrange platters of seafood and bowls of dip on the table.

Fill a metal fondue pot no more than one-third full with the oil. Put the pot on the stovetop and heat the oil to 190°C/375°F or until a cube of bread browns in 30 seconds. Very carefully transfer the pot to the tabletop burner.

Invite guests to cook the skewers in the hot oil for about 1 minute, then roll the skewers in the almond and basil dip and eat. Note that when the squid is added to the pot of hot oil, it can spit a lot so take care not to burn yourself.

STOCK
FONDUE

POACHED CHINESE CHICKEN

WITH BOK CHOY & CRISPY SHALLOTS

200 g/7 oz. shiitake mushrooms, stems removed

3 baby bok choy, halved and thickly sliced

200 g/7 oz. choi sum, cut into small pieces/florets

4 spring onions/scallions, thinly sliced

4 small handfuls of coriander/cilantro leaves

sticky rice, crispy shallots and chilli/chili sauce, to serve

BROTH

1.5 kg/3¼ lb. free-range chicken

250 ml/1 cup Shaoxing rice wine

1 bunch of spring onions/scallions, trimmed and chopped

8 garlic cloves, roughly chopped

5-cm/2-in. piece of root ginger, sliced and bruised

1 teaspoon salt

a few black peppercorns

SOY & SESAME DIPPING SAUCE

200 ml/¾ cup dark soy sauce

120 ml/½ cup broth

1 tablespoon sesame oil

2 teaspoons caster/granulated sugar

SERVES 6–8

This recipe is based on a classic southern Chinese dish of chicken simply poached in a fragrant broth and dressed with soy sauce, coriander/cilantro and spring onions/scallions. Start this dish a day ahead.

To make the broth, cut the chicken into quarters so there are 2 breast/wing quarters and 2 leg/drumstick quarters. Using poultry shears and a sharp knife, separate the wing section from each breast and place the wings in a large saucepan. Carefully fillet the chicken breasts from the carcass and set aside, add the carcass to the pan. Joint the thighs and drumsticks from each other, then using a large knife and a meat mallet, cut through the bone of both the drumsticks and thighs into 3-cm/1¼-in. pieces. Cut each chicken breast fillet into 3-cm/1¼-in. pieces. (Alternatively, either ask your butcher to do this for you or use ready filleted chicken thighs and breast and cut these up, but you will need to flavour your broth with either a roast chicken carcass or a good-quality chicken stock cube.) Cover and refrigerate.

Add the remaining broth ingredients and 3 litres/quarts water to the pan containing the wings and carcass. Bring to the boil, skim the surface to remove any scum and simmer gently for 1 hour, then remove from the heat. Cool the broth, then strain through a fine sieve into your fondue pan. Refrigerate overnight.

The next day carefully remove the fat from the surface. Return the broth to the heat and bring to the boil. Simmer for about 15 minutes or until approximately 1.25 litres/5 cups remain.

Combine the sauce ingredients in a bowl and stir until the sugar is dissolved, then divide between small bowls.

Arrange the chicken pieces, remaining ingredients and all the accompaniments in bowls or on plates on the table.

Return the broth to the boil and carefully transfer it to the tabletop burner. Add the chicken thigh and leg pieces on the bone to the broth with the shiitake and simmer for about 5 minutes. Then add the chicken breast pieces, bok choy and choi sum and cook for 3 minutes or until the chicken is tender and thoroughly cooked, then serve with the accompaniments.

CHICKEN IN VINE LEAVES

WITH LEMON-SCENTED BROTH

6 boneless, skinless chicken
   breasts
3 red or yellow (bell) peppers
125 g/4½ oz. preserved vine
   leaves, about 24, drained

LEMON-SCENTED BROTH
500 g/1 lb. 2 oz. chicken wings
3 garlic cloves
1 onion, halved
2 bay leaves
½ tablespoon black peppercorns
a large bunch of parsley, 25 g/1 oz.
1 preserved lemon, washed,
   deseeded and finely chopped
sea salt

TO SERVE
boiled rice
selection of sauces, such as
   tapenade, tzatziki, hummus,
   pesto, tomato salsa and/or
   sweet chilli

SERVES 6

Wrapping chicken in vine leaves not only infuses the chicken with flavour, it also looks more stylish. The preserved lemons bring a wonderfully intense flavour to the dish, but you can substitute lemon zest if necessary.

To make the broth, put all the broth ingredients except the lemon and salt into a large saucepan. Add 2 litres/quarts water, bring to the boil, reduce to a simmer and cook for 45 minutes, skimming off any foam that forms on the top. Strain into a metal fondue pot. Remove any meat from the chicken bones, shred, then add to the stock. Discard the bones. Add the preserved lemon and salt to taste and enough water to fill the pot two-thirds full.

Butterfly each chicken breast by slicing through to about 1 cm/½ in. from the edge and opening out. Using a meat mallet or rolling pin, gently flatten the chicken to 1 cm/½ in. thick.

Roast the (bell) peppers under a very hot grill/broiler or in the flames of a gas burner, until blackened all over. Transfer to a large bowl and cover with clingfilm/plastic wrap. Let steam for about 10 minutes, then peel off the skin. Split the peppers into quarters and discard the stalks and seeds.

Arrange 4 vine leaves in an overlapping square. Top with a piece of chicken and 2 quarters of pepper. Roll up tightly and slice into 6 rounds, like sushi. Secure each piece with a long skewer, sliding the chicken about a quarter of the way up the skewer. Repeat until all the chicken has been used, the refrigerate until needed.

Return the broth to the boil and carefully transfer it to the tabletop burner. Invite your guests to dip the rolls into the broth and cook for 5–6 minutes or until the chicken s cooked through. Serve with rice and sauces.

DUCK LAKSA BROTH

250 g/9 oz. dried rice stick noodles
2 small duck breast fillets (about 650 g/1 lb. 7 oz.)
2 tablespoons vegetable oil
4 lime leaves, torn
2 star anise, lightly bashed
1 cinnamon stick, lightly bashed
2 Thai red chillies/chiles, lightly bashed
400 ml/1¾ cups coconut milk
1 litre/quart chicken stock
3 tablespoons fish sauce
1 tablespoon caster/granulated sugar
250 g/9 oz. deep-fried puffed tofu (or plain tofu)
sambal oelek, shredded vegetables, lime wedges, Asian herbs and crispy shallots, to serve

LAKSA PASTE
2 teaspoons coriander seeds
6 small shallots, chopped
4 garlic cloves, chopped
2 stalks lemongrass, thinly sliced
2 Thai red chillies/chiles, seeded and chopped
5-cm/2-in. piece of fresh turmeric, peeled and chopped (or 1 teaspoon ground turmeric)
2.5-cm/1-in. piece of galangal, peeled and chopped
4 macadamia nuts, roughly chopped
1 tablespoon shrimp paste

SERVES 4

Laksa is a Malaysian spice paste mix used in many traditional recipes. The addition of turmeric is typical of Malaysian cuisine due to the influence of Indian migrants who brought many of their foods and culinary traditions with them. Used in a variety of different recipes, laksa is best known as a noodle soup that is named after it; it is the turmeric that gives it that deep yellow/ochre colour. When cooking the broth on the stovetop you can use a wok or deep frying pan/skillet at this stage and then transfer it to the fondue pot once ready to serve, if preferred.

Make the laksa paste. Dry fry the coriander seeds in a small frying pan/skillet until golden, cool and grind to a fine powder using a spice grinder. Place all the ingredients along with the ground coriander in a blender and blitz together until the paste is as smooth as possible. Transfer to a container and set aside until required (this can be made several days ahead and stored in the fridge; this recipe makes approximately double the amount of paste you need but leftovers can be kept in the fridge for at least a month).

Soak the noodles in hot water according to the packet instructions (usually 15–20 minutes). Drain well but leave in the colander/strainer until required, covered with a kitchen towel.

Carefully remove the skin from the duck and discard. Thinly slice the breast into 2-mm/⅛-in. thick slices and place on a large platter, cover and set aside.

Meanwhile, heat the oil in the fondue pot on the stovetop and add 4 tablespoons of the laksa paste. Fry for 2 minutes until fragrant, then add the lime leaves, star anise, cinnamon stick, red chillies/chiles, coconut milk, chicken stock, fish sauce and sugar. Simmer gently for 10 minutes and keep warm.

Arrange all the accompaniments in bowls on the table with the puffed tofu and sliced duck. Pour a little boiling water over the noodles to warm them through and divide between 4 warmed soup bowls. Return the broth to the boil and carefully transfer it to the tabletop burner. Diners can then add the duck slices and puffed tofu to the broth and cook for about 2 minutes until the duck is tender, hot and cooked. Ladle into your noodle bowls, add all the different accompaniments and eat at once.

POACHED BEEF FILLET

WITH ANCHOVY & CELERIAC

500 g/1 lb. 2 oz. piece beef fillet
150 g/5½ oz. peeled celeriac/
   celery root
1 large crisp eating apple
50 g/½ cup toasted walnuts,
   roughly chopped
a handful of fresh parsley leaves
1 bunch of watercress
2 tablespoons drained baby capers
freshly squeezed lemon juice
walnut oil

BROTH
4 tablespoons olive oil
1.5 kg/3¼ lb. beef blade,
   cut into chunks
2 large onions, chopped
2 large carrots, chopped
2 large celery sticks, chopped
4 large garlic cloves
2 sprigs of fresh thyme
2 bay leaves
2 teaspoons salt
a few black peppercorns

ANCHOVY DRESSING
1 egg yolk
10 anchovies in oil (about 50 g/
   2 oz.), drained and chopped
2 teaspoons white wine vinegar
1 teaspoon Dijon mustard
50 ml/3½ tablespoons extra virgin
   olive oil
4 tablespoons single/light cream
salt and freshly ground
   black pepper

SERVES 4

Start this recipe a day ahead to make the rich beef broth. The next day, the reheated stock is placed on the fondue burner at the table, so diners can poach the beef fillet either as a whole piece or in half for just a few minutes to seal the outside and leave the beef beautifully rare and tender. It is then sliced, in the same way as carpaccio of beef, and served with a crisp salad of celeriac/celery root, apple and walnuts and a creamy anchovy dressing.

To make the broth, heat the oil in a large saucepan on the stovetop and fry the blade in several batches until well browned, then return them to the pan. Add 3 litres/quarts of cold water with all remaining broth ingredients and bring to the boil, skimming to remove any scum. Partially cover the pan and simmer gently for 2 hours or until the stock is full of flavour. Check the seasoning.

Strain the broth through a fine sieve/strainer and leave to cool (discard the beef blade). Once cold, transfer the broth to the fridge overnight. The next day, remove from the fridge and discard the thick layer of fat from the surface of the broth. Bring it to the boil on the stovetop.

To make the dressing, place the egg yolk, anchovies, vinegar, mustard and a little pepper in a blender and blend until smooth. Gradually whisk in the oil, then the cream, keeping the motor running until the sauce is thickened. Cover and set aside.

To make the salad, thinly pare the celeriac/celery root and cut into matchsticks. Cut the apple into the same size sticks and place in a bowl with the walnuts, parsley, watercress and capers. Add a little lemon juice and walnut oil to taste, plus salt and pepper as necessary.

Season the beef fillet and depending on the size of your fondue pot, either leave whole or cut in half crossways.

Return the broth to the boil and carefully transfer it to the tabletop burner. Carefully immerse the beef fillet into the pan, making sure it is covered with stock. Simmer for 2–3 minutes, then remove the beef using a slotted spoon. Pat dry with kitchen paper and place on a wooden board. Cut into thin slices, drizzle over the anchovy dressing and serve with the salad. Allow the stock to cool and freeze for a later date.

BEEF WITH HORSERADISH

IN RED WINE & JUNIPER STOCK

1.25 kg/2¾ lb beef fillet, finely sliced
toasted rye bread, sour cream and
  parsley leaves, to serve

RED WINE & JUNIPER STOCK
1 kg/2 lb. 4 oz. beef bones
1 onion, coarsely chopped
2 carrots, coarsely chopped
1 celery stalk
250 ml/1 cup red wine
1 tablespoon juniper berries
½ teaspoon whole cloves
2–3 whole star anise
1 teaspoon black peppercorns
sea salt

BEETROOT & HORSERADISH RELISH
3 beetroot/beets, raw and unpeeled,
  scrubbed well
1 tablespoon olive oil
1½ tablespoons horseradish sauce
sea salt and freshly ground
  black pepper

SERVES 6

The beef is prepared in the same way as Fondue Bourguignonne on page 115 – freeze the fillet for 2–3 hours first to make it easier to slice thinly. The stock is delicious: if you have any left over, it can be used in soups and it also freezes very well. If fresh beetroot/beets are not available, the canned kind makes a speedy substitute.

To make the stock, preheat the oven to 200°C/fan 180°C/400°F/Gas 6. Put the beef bones into a roasting pan and cook in the preheated oven for 30 minutes. Remove and transfer to a large saucepan. Add the onion, carrots, celery and 3 litres/quarts water and bring to the boil. Simmer for 1 hour, skimming any foam that forms on the surface. Strain and discard the solids.

To make the relish, preheat the oven to 180°C/fan 160°C/350°F/Gas 4. Put the beetroot/beets into a roasting pan and cook in the preheated oven for 40 minutes or until tender. Cool slightly and peel. Grate coarsely into a bowl and stir in the olive oil, horseradish sauce, salt and pepper.

Put the red wine into a metal fondue pot and bring to the boil on the stovetop. Boil until reduced by half, then add the juniper berries, cloves, star anise, peppercorns and strained stock. Add salt to taste. Return the broth to the boil and carefully transfer it to the tabletop burner.

Put platters of sliced beef and toasted rye bread, a bowl of relish, sour cream and parsley leaves on the table. Invite guests to thread a slice of beef onto a fondue fork and cook in the simmering stock for 30–60 seconds. Eat the beef on the toasted bread with a spoonful of the beetroot and horseradish relish, sour cream and some parsley.

THAI-STYLE SEAFOOD STEAMBOAT

400 g/14 oz. rice vermicelli
 noodles
sesame oil
400 g/14 oz. skinless white fish,
 such as monkfish, cod
 or haddock
500 g/1 lb. 2 oz. small clams
 or mussels, scrubbed
400 g/14 oz. calamari bodies

BROTH
20 large raw prawns/shrimp
2 litres/quarts chicken or fish
 stock
4 garlic cloves, roughly chopped
2 red bird's eye chillies/chiles,
 bruised
6 makrut lime leaves, bruised
2.5-cm/1-in. piece of galangal,
 sliced and bruised
2 stalks lemongrass, trimmed
 and bruised
4 tablespoons fish sauce
3 tablespoons freshly squeezed
 lime juice
3 tablespoons palm sugar
1–2 tablespoons light soy sauce,
 to taste
2 tomatoes, diced

TO GARNISH
garlic and ginger sauce (see Note)
soy, sesame and chilli/chile sauce
 (see Tip)
a handful of beansprouts for
 each serving
handfuls of fresh Thai basil,
 mint and coriander/cilantro
a bowl of crispy fried shallots

SERVES 4–6

The steamboat was introduced into northern China by nomadic Mongolian herders who used their helmets to cook a broth of meat and roots over a campfire. The Chinese adapted the original dish and its popularity as a cooking method spread. I had my most memorable steamboat in Thailand – the aromatic broth was served in a classic aluminium hotpot, with seafood, noodles, vegetables, herbs and aromatics all piled high. The already delicious broth became richer and more intense the more ingredients we cooked in it.

To make the broth, peel the heads and shells from the prawns/shrimp, reserving the bodies. Place the shells and heads into a large saucepan with the stock, garlic, chillies/chiles, lime leaves, galangal and lemongrass and bring to the boil. Simmer gently for 10 minutes until fragrant, then strain the stock into a clean pan. Stir in the fish sauce, lime juice, palm sugar, soy sauce and tomatoes and simmer for 5 minutes. Set aside.

Soak the noodles in boiling water for 10–15 minutes (depending on the brand) until al dente, then drain, toss with a little sesame oil and set aside. To prepare the seafood, remove the intestinal tract from the back of each prawn/shrimp, wash gently and pat dry. Cube the fish, scrub the clam shells and cut the calamari into bite-sized pieces. Arrange all the ingredients on plates or in bowls, including all the garnishes and accompaniments.

Return the broth to the boil and carefully transfer it to the tabletop burner. Using tongs or slotted spoons, cook the seafood in the hot stock. Divide the noodles between the bowls, adding the seafood as it cooks along with all the garnishes. Discard any shellfish that has not opened during cooking.

Note To make the ginger and garlic sauce, combine 75 ml/ 5 tablespoons fish sauce, 2 tablespoons water, 1 tablespoon freshly grated ginger, 2 crushed garlic cloves, 2 tablespoons rice wine vinegar and a pinch of sugar, stirring to dissolve the sugar.

To make the soy, sesame and chilli sauce, combine 100 ml/ 7 tablespoons light soy sauce, 1 tablespoon freshly grated ginger, 1–2 sliced red chillies/chiles, 2 teaspoons sesame oil and 1 tablespoon caster/granulated sugar, stirring to dissolve the sugar.

POACHED LANGOUSTINES WITH MAYONNAISE

1.5 kg/3¼ lb. raw langoustines or
   large raw prawns/jumbo shrimp
1 kg/2¼ lb. fish trimmings
750-ml bottle dry white wine
1 leek, sliced
2 garlic cloves
½ bunch fresh dill
1 teaspoon sea salt
a few black peppercorns
bread and butter, to serve

BASIC MAYONNAISE
3 egg yolks
2 teaspoons white wine vinegar
1 teaspoon Dijon mustard
300 ml/1¼ cups olive oil

PERNOD MAYONNAISE
125 ml/½ cup basic mayonnaise
2 teaspoons freshly squeezed
   lemon juice
2 teaspoons Pernod

MARIE ROSE MAYONNAISE
125 ml/½ cup basic mayonnaise
2 tablespoons tomato ketchup
1 teaspoon Worcestershire sauce
a squeeze of fresh lemon juice

GREEN GODDESS MAYONNAISE
125 ml/½ cup basic mayonnaise
2 tablespoons chopped mixed fresh
   herbs, such as parsley, tarragon
   and chives
1 white anchovy fillet in oil, drained
   and chopped
1 spring onion/scallion, trimmed
   and chopped
1 small garlic clove, crushed
2 tablespoons full-fat/whole milk
1 tablespoon white wine vinegar
salt and freshly ground black pepper

SERVES 4

A very simple classic dish. Langoustines (also known as scampi or Dublin Bay prawns) have a lovely sweetness of flavour, especially when really fresh. You can buy them from good quality fishmongers or if you are unable to find any, this recipe works equally as well with large raw prawns/jumbo shrimp. Follow the same method.

Make the broth. Carefully pull the langoustine heads from the bodies and place the heads only in a saucepan with 2 litres/quarts of cold water and all the remaining broth ingredients. Bring to the boil, skim the surface to remove any scum and simmer gently, partially covered for 30 minutes. Strain the broth through a fine sieve into the fondue pot and return the liquid to the boil. Simmer for 15 minutes or until you have about 1 litre/4 cups of broth remaining.

Meanwhile, carefully snip down the back of each langoustine body and into the flesh a little way to expose the black intestinal tract and discard this (I use a cocktail stick/toothpick to tease it out). Gently wash the langoustines, pat dry and keep in a cool place until required.

Make the basic mayonnaise. Place the egg yolks, vinegar, mustard and a little salt and pepper in a bowl and using electric beaters, whisk until the mixture is frothy. Then very gradually whisk in the oil, a little at a time, whisking well after each addition until the sauce is thick and glossy and all the oil incorporated.

Divide the mayonnaise into thirds and add the different flavourings. The green goddess dressing will need to be blitzed in a blender until it is smooth.

Return the broth to the boil and carefully transfer it to the tabletop burner. Diners can then pop the langoustines into the broth for 1–2 minutes until cooked. Allow to cool for a moment or two until they are cool enough to handle and pull the bodies from the shells.

Serve with the mayonnaises and some buttered bread. Keep the remaining broth at the end of the meal and freeze it once cold to use as a stock at a later date.

RASAM
WITH SALMON & INDIAN-STYLE BROTH

2 tablespoons ghee or butter
2 teaspoons yellow or brown
    mustard seeds
1 teaspoon cumin seeds
4 x 200-g/7-oz. trout or salmon
    fillets, skinned and cut into
    3-cm/1¼-in. pieces
200 g/1½ cups fresh or
    frozen peas
4 plum tomatoes, cut into
    bite-sized pieces
poppadoms and lime pickle,
    to serve

TURMERIC POTATOES
50 g/3½ tablespoons ghee
    or butter
750 g/1 lb. 10 oz. potatoes, cubed
1½ teaspoons ground turmeric
½ teaspoon garam masala
2 tablespoons coriander/
    cilantro leaves

RASAM PASTE
3 tablespoons tamarind paste
3 ripe tomatoes, roughly chopped
4 garlic cloves, roughly chopped
a handful of curry leaves or
    coriander/cilantro stalks
1½ teaspoons coriander seeds
¼ teaspoon black peppercorns
2 teaspoons sea salt

SERVES 4

Rasam – a spiced tomato and tamarind soup – is a traditional South Indian food. It is made with tamarind paste as a base, with the addition of tomato, chilli/chili powder, pepper, garlic, curry leaves, mustard, cumin, coriander/cilantro and salt. It can be served on its own or as part of a larger meal. I have adapted this version to work in a hotpot, serving it with salmon and delicious turmeric potatoes.

To make the rasam paste, place all the ingredients in a blender and blitz until smooth.

For the broth, heat the ghee in a fondue pot or saucepan on the stovetop and fry the mustard seeds and cumin seeds for 2 minutes until really fragrant, then add the rasam paste. Fry over a medium heat for 4–5 minutes or until the paste is thickened. Add 1 litre/quart of water and the curry leaves or coriander/cilantro stalks and bring to the boil. Simmer gently for 10 minutes. Keep warm.

To cook the potatoes, melt the ghee or butter in a frying pan/skillet and fry the potatoes over a medium heat for 10 minutes, then stir in the turmeric, garam masala and some salt and pepper. Partially cover and cook for a further 10 minutes or until the potatoes are cooked and tender. Using a fork, mash them lightly until 'smashed'. Add the coriander/cilantro leaves.

Place the fish, peas and tomatoes into small bowls and arrange on the table. Place the potatoes on the table, still in the frying pan/skillet. Return the broth to the boil and carefully transfer it to the tabletop burner. Diners can now add the salmon and tomatoes and cook for 2 minutes before adding the peas for a minute or so until cooked. Divide the potatoes between warmed serving bowls and spoon over the fish, vegetables and some of the delicious broth. Serve with poppadoms and lime pickle if wished.

FISH & SEAFOOD
IN SAFFRON & TOMATO BROTH

12 uncooked tiger prawns/
   shrimp peeled
12 scallops
500 g/1 lb. 2 oz. monkfish,
   cut into bite-sized chunks
500 g/1 lb. 2 oz. salmon fillet,
   cut into bite-sized chunks
crusty bread, to serve

SAFFRON & TOMATO BROTH
1 tablespoon olive oil
2 garlic cloves, sliced
1 onion, sliced
1 red chilli/chile, deseeded
   and sliced
500 g/1 lb. 2 oz. tomatoes,
   finely chopped
2 anchovy fillets, chopped
   (optional)
250 ml/1 cup dry white wine
2 bay leaves
1 long piece of orange peel,
   fresh or dried
¼ teaspoon saffron threads,
   soaked in 4 tablespoons
   boiling water for 15 minutes
sea salt and freshly ground
   black pepper

ROUILLE
1 thick slice of baguette
1 egg yolk
2 garlic cloves, crushed
¼ teaspoon saffron powder
½ teaspoon finely chopped
   fresh chilli/chile
4 tablespoons olive oil

SERVES 6

Hot stock is a wonderful cooking medium for seafood – this one is infused with saffron and tomato to give a delicious broth packed with Mediterranean flavour.

To make the broth, put the oil into a large saucepan and heat gently. Add the garlic, onion and chilli/chile and sauté for a few minutes. Add the tomatoes, anchovies, white wine, bay leaves, orange peel and 250 ml/1 cup water and bring to the boil. Let simmer for 20 minutes, then add the saffron and its soaking water and simmer for a further 10 minutes.

To make the rouille, moisten the baguette with a little broth. Put it into small food processor, then add the egg yolk, garlic, saffron and chilli/chile and blend well. With the machine running, slowly pour in the oil to form a paste, then add 1–2 teaspoons of the broth and stir well. Transfer the rouille to 6 small bowls.

Purée the broth in a blender and then pass through a sieve/strainer into a metal fondue pot until two-thirds full, adding extra water if necessary. Season with salt and pepper and return to the boil. Return the broth to the boil and carefully transfer it to the tabletop burner.

Invite guests to spear pieces of fish and shellfish with their fondue forks, lower into the boiling broth and cook for 30–60 seconds. Serve with rouille and crusty bread. The broth can be served as a soup, either after the fondue or next day.

LOBSTER & SOLE

IN ANISE-SCENTED COURT BOUILLON

The aniseed flavours of Pernod and chervil complement the delicate lobster and sole in this hotpot-style fondue. If you can't get lobster, try langoustine, scallops or another firm white fish. Using the lobster shells in the court bouillon will give it exceptional flavour.

2 small sole fillets, skinned, about 700 g/1 lb. 9 oz.
a small bunch of chervil
about 500 g/1 lb. 2 oz. lobster tails, with shell if possible, prawns/ shrimp or scallops, or monkfish, cut into bite-sized pieces (I used a whole 500-g/1 lb. 2-oz. lobster, cut the tail into 4 pieces and cracked the claw shell to expose the meat, plus 4 large prawns/ jumbo shrimp)

PERNOD COURT BOUILLON
2 tablespoons olive oil
2 small carrots, finely chopped
1 celery stalk, finely chopped
1 small leek, sliced
1 bay leaf
a small bunch of parsley
1 tablespoon fennel seeds
750 g/1 lb. 10 oz. fish trimmings, including lobster or langoustine shells if possible
60 ml/4 tablespoons Pernod
salt

TO SERVE
boiled new potatoes
green salad
lemon mayonnaise or melted butter

SERVES 6

To make the court bouillon, put the oil into a large saucepan, heat gently, then add the carrots, celery and leek and sauté until soft, about 5 minutes. Add 2 litres/quarts water, the bay leaf, parsley, fennel seeds and fish trimmings and any lobster, langoustine or prawn/shrimp heads. Simmer for 30 minutes.

Meanwhile, cut the sole fillets in half lengthways. Put a tiny bunch of chervil at the end of each and roll up. Secure each roll with a long skewer. Spear the pieces of lobster onto skewers. Place on a platter.

Strain the court bouillon into a metal fondue pot, add enough water to fill the pot two-thirds full, then bring to the boil on the stovetop. Add the Pernod and salt to taste. Return the broth to the boil and carefully transfer it to the tabletop burner.

Invite guests to cook the lobster and sole rolls in the boiling stock for 30–60 seconds. Suitable accompaniments, especially for an elegant summer meal, are boiled new potatoes, a green salad and some lemon mayonnaise or melted butter for dipping.

SWEET FONDUE

BABA BUNS

WITH CARAMELIZED ORANGE SAUCE

1½ teaspoons dried active yeast
60 ml/4 tablespoons warm milk
2 tablespoons caster/granulated
    sugar
300 g/2¼ cups plain/all-purpose
    flour
a pinch of salt
3 medium eggs, beaten
60 g/4 tablespoons unsalted
    butter, softened, plus extra
    for greasing
pomegranate seeds, to serve

CARAMELIZED ORANGE SAUCE
8 small oranges
250 ml/1 cup freshly squeezed
    orange juice
100 g/½ cup caster/granulated
    sugar
4 tablespoons golden syrup/
    corn syrup
100 g/7 tablespoons unsalted
    butter
100 ml/⅓ cup plus 1 tablespoon
    double/heavy cream
1 tablespoon orange flower water
a pinch of sea salt

8 x 150-ml/⅔-cup timbales

SERVES 8

Rum baba, a brioche-like dessert soaked in rum, is a French classic. Here the little buns are cooked, and rather than a rum syrup being poured over whilst hot, these are cooled and served with a fragrant orange sauce, either to dip or to drizzle.

To make the babas, whisk the yeast into the warm milk along with the sugar and leave for 10 minutes until frothy. Sift the flour and salt into the bowl of a food mixer and add the frothed yeast mixture and eggs and bring together to form a sticky dough. Knead on a low speed for 2–3 minutes until it is starting to look elastic, then gradually beat in the butter a little at a time until all is incorporated. The mixture is very wet, more like a sponge batter than a bread dough. Cover the bowl with clingfilm/plastic wrap and leave to rise for 1–1½ hours until doubled in size.

Butter the timbales. Using a spoon, scoop out the risen dough and divide equally between the timbales. Using wet hands, smooth the surface flat and press down a little to remove air bubbles. Cover with oiled clingfilm/plastic wrap and leave to rise for a further 30 minutes until the dough reaches the top of the timbales.

Preheat the oven to 170°C/fan 150°C/325°F/Gas 3.

Remove the clingfilm/plastic wrap and transfer the timbales to the preheated oven. Cook for 20 minutes until well risen and lightly golden. Cool in the timbales for 5 minutes, then turn out and cool on a wire rack.

Meanwhile, make the sauce. Peel 4 of the oranges, holding them over a small saucepan to catch any juices. Squeeze the juice from the remaining oranges into the pan – you need 250 ml/1 cup juice, so make it up with a little water if necessary. Add the sugar and golden syrup/corn syrup to the saucepan and heat, stirring, until the sugar dissolves. Bring to the boil and cook without stirring for about 10 minutes until the sauce is thickened and starting to turn a slightly darker colour. Carefully stir in the butter until melted and then the cream, and simmer for a further 3–4 minutes until thickened to the consistency of double/heavy cream. Stir in the orange flower water.

Cut the peeled oranges into thin slices and divide between serving plates with the babas and pomegranate seeds. Transfer the sauce to the tabletop burner. Cut the babas into slices or chunks and dip into the sauce.

FROZEN SUMMER BERRIES

WITH WHITE CHOCOLATE CUSTARD

300 ml/1¼ cups full-fat/
  whole milk
250 ml/1 cup double/heavy cream
1 vanilla pod/bean, split
5 egg yolks
2 tablespoons caster/
  granulated sugar
2 teaspoons cornflour/cornstarch
150 g/5½ oz. white chocolate,
  chopped
500 g/1 lb. 2 oz. mixed frozen
  summer berries

MERINGUE KISSES
2 egg whites
60 g/5 tablespoons caster/
  granulated sugar
a pinch of salt
a few drops of vanilla extract

SERVES 4

Inspired by a dessert at the Ivy restaurant in central London, this dessert of frozen summer berries is warmed with a hot white chocolate sauce poured over it immediately before serving. With the pouring done at the table by the waiter, the dish had a touch of drama about it, much like the place itself with its clientele of actors and such like. Of course, I couldn't resist it on my first and only meal there and although so simple (as was much of the menu, but done well) it was really very lovely – the warmth of the sauce caressing the berries and softening them, whilst retaining a delightful cool crispness, was wonderful. Here is my version served with meringue kisses.

First make the meringue kisses. Preheat the oven to 120°C/fan 100°C/250°F/Gas ½ and line a baking sheet with baking paper.

Whisk the egg whites in a bowl until foamy, then add the sugar a spoonful at a time and mix until the mixture is thickened and glossy. Finally, whisk in the salt and vanilla extract. Spoon or pipe small 2-cm/¾-in. rounds of meringue onto the prepared baking sheet and bake in the preheated oven for 35–40 minutes until the kisses are set. Remove from the oven and cool on the trays. Store in an airtight container.

Make the sauce. Heat the milk, cream and vanilla pod/bean together in a saucepan set over a gentle heat until it reaches boiling point, then remove from the heat and set aside to infuse for 20 minutes. Discard the vanilla pod/bean.

Whisk the egg yolks, sugar and cornflour/cornstarch together in a bowl until pale and creamy, then stir in the infused milk. Pour the custard into your fondue pot and on the stovetop, heat gently, stirring constantly, until the mixture thickens to coat the back of the spoon. Remove the pan from the heat and gradually stir in the chocolate until melted. Transfer the fondue pot to the tabletop burner.

Remove the berries from the freezer and spoon into bowls or glasses. Diners can now ladle the hot sauce directly from the pot on to the frozen berries, allowing them to melt and soften just a little. Serve with the meringue kisses.

DOUGHNUTS

WITH SALTED BOURBON CARAMEL

2 teaspoons dried active yeast
125 ml/½ cup warmed milk
2 tablespoons caster/granulated sugar, plus extra for dusting
375 g/2⅔ cups unbleached white bread flour, plus extra for dusting
1 teaspoon vanilla extract
15 g/1 tablespoon unsalted butter, melted
2 medium eggs, beaten
sunflower or vegetable oil, for frying

SALTED BOURBON CARAMEL SAUCE
250 g/9 oz. milk chocolate, chopped
60 g/4 tablespoons unsalted butter
60 g/5 tablespoons light muscovado sugar
60 ml/4 tablespoons double/heavy cream
1 tablespoon bourbon or whisky
a pinch of sea salt

10-cm/4-in. doughnut ring or round cookie cutter

SERVES 8

I always thought doughnuts were something you only ever bought, not made at home. Then I tried and found them easy to make and wonderfully light, fluffy and far less oily than shop-made ones, and I could sugar them or dunk them into a yummy sauce. It is best to eat these as hot as you can after cooking, so work your timings back from serving and it should be no problem at all.

To make the doughnuts, place the yeast and warm milk in a bowl with a pinch of the sugar and 1 tablespoon flour. Stir well to dissolve the yeast and set aside to froth for 10 minutes. Sift the remaining flour into a large bowl and make a well in the middle. Add the frothed yeast mixture, vanilla extract, melted butter and egg and work the mixture together with your hands to form a fairly sticky dough. Cover the bowl with clingfilm/plastic wrap and rest for 15 minutes.

Knead the dough on a well-floured surface for 5 minutes until smooth. Shape it into a ball and place in a lightly oiled bowl. Cover and leave to rise for 1 hour or until doubled in size.

Very gently, remove the risen dough from the bowl and using your fingers, press to form a 1.5-cm/⅝-in. thick rectangle. Using the doughnut ring or cookie cutter, stamp out as many doughnuts as you can. (You can re-roll the dough to stamp out more, but I prefer to simply fry the odds and ends left over from the doughnut rings.)

To make the sauce, place the chocolate, butter and sugar in a fondue pot and heat gently on the stovetop, stirring constantly, until melted. Whisk in the cream and cook for 2–3 minutes until the sauce has thickened. Remove from the heat and allow the bubbles to subside, then stir in the bourbon and salt. Transfer the fondue pot to the tabletop burner on a low setting to keep warm.

Heat 5 cm/2 in. of oil in a heavy saucepan until it reaches 180°C/350°F. Fry the doughnuts in two batches for 3 minutes, turning halfway through, until they are puffed up and golden. Drain immediately on kitchen paper, dust with sugar if you wish and keep warm in the oven. Arrange the doughnuts on a plate for diners to spear and dunk into the salted bourbon caramel sauce (any leftover sauce can be kept in the fridge for a week).

SMOKED CHILLI-CHOCOLATE FONDUE
WITH WAFFLES

150 ml/²/₃ cup double/heavy cream
250 g/9 oz. dark chocolate, chopped
¼ teaspoon smoked paprika
a pinch of chilli/hot red pepper flakes
1 tablespoon Pedro Ximénez
  or sweet dark sherry
double/heavy cream and strawberries,
  raspberries or blueberries, to serve

WAFFLES
150 g/1 cup plus 2 tablespoons plain/
  all-purpose flour
1 teaspoon baking powder
½ teaspoon bicarbonate of soda/
  baking soda
1 tablespoon caster/granulated sugar
125 ml/½ cup buttermilk
1 egg, lightly beaten
75 g/5 tablespoons butter, melted
icing/confectioner's sugar, for dusting

waffle iron

SERVES 6

The addition of a little smoked paprika as well as chilli/hot red pepper flakes to the chocolate brings a hint of intrigue to this sauce, while a dash of Pedro Ximénez – a velvety rich, sweet sherry – brings a further depth of flavour. Served with lightly fluffy waffles, it is quite something. If you can't lay a hand on a waffle maker, don't worry as a simple sandwich maker or even a frying pan/skillet can be used; they will end up a little more like hotcakes as they would require flipping but the flavour is the same.

Prepare the fondue. Place the cream, chocolate, smoked paprika, chilli/hot red pepper flakes and sherry into a small saucepan and heat very gently on the stovetop, stirring, until the chocolate is melted. Keep warm.

To make the waffles, sift the flour, baking powder and bicarbonate of soda/baking soda into a bowl. Stir in the sugar. Beat the remaining ingredients together and then beat them into the dry ingredients until smooth. Spoon a layer of the batter into a heated waffle iron and spread flat. Cook for about 2 minutes until puffed up, crisp and golden. Remove the waffle and repeat to use up all the batter (there is enough batter to make 6–8 waffles, but sometimes the first waffle doesn't come out too well).

Transfer the fondue pot to the tabletop burner and serve the waffles lightly dusted with icing/confectioner's sugar with cream, your favourite fruits and drizzled with the delicious smoky chocolate sauce.

Note The sauce recipe makes more than you are likely to need for this dish but it keeps well in a jar in the fridge for up to 1 week or can be frozen for up to 3 months.

BITTER CHOCOLATE FONDUE
WITH CHURROS

300 g/10½ oz. dark/bittersweet
   chocolate
125 ml/½ cup double/heavy cream
¼ teaspoon dried chilli/hot
   red pepper flakes (optional)
2 tablespoons orange liqueur
   such as Cointreau (optional)
finely grated zest and juice
   of 2 oranges

CHURROS
120 g/½ cup plus 2 teaspoons
   butter
150 g/1 cup plus 2 tablespoons
   plain/all-purpose flour,
   twice sifted
a pinch of salt
3 medium eggs, beaten
75 g/6 tablespoons caster/
   granulated sugar
2 teaspoons ground cinnamon
vegetable oil, for frying

a strong piping/pastry bag fitted
   with a 1-cm/½-in. star nozzle

SERVES 6

Sweet fondues served at the end of a meal make an easy, friendly dessert. Any sweet biscuits or cookies are good for dipping, but churros – the delicious doughnuts the Spanish serve with hot chocolate – work exceptionally well.

To make the churros, heat 250 ml/1 cup cold water and the butter in a saucepan over a low heat until the butter melts. Tip in the flour and salt and beat well with a wooden spoon until the mixture comes away from the pan edges. Cool for 5 minutes. Whisk in the eggs a little at a time, using electric beaters, until you have a smooth batter. Spoon into a piping/pastry bag fitted with a 1-cm/½-in. star nozzle.

Pour vegetable oil into a heavy-based saucepan to a depth of 5 cm/2 in. and heat until it reaches 180°C/350°F. Carefully pipe 12-cm/5-in. lengths of the dough straight into the hot oil, using scissors to cut the dough. Fry 3 churros at a time for 2–3 minutes until crisp and golden, turning halfway through using metal tongs. Remove with a slotted spoon and drain on paper towels.

Combine the sugar and cinnamon on a plate and roll the churros in the mixture until coated.

To prepare the fondue, put the chocolate into the top of a double boiler, add the cream, chilli/hot red pepper flakes, liqueur, if using, and orange zest and juice. Heat over simmering water and stir until the sauce is melted and smooth. Transfer to a warmed fondue pot set over its tabletop burner. Serve with the churros for dipping.

MASCARPONE & ROSE FONDUE
WITH ALMOND SYRUP BISCUITS

300 g/10$\frac{1}{2}$ oz. mascarpone
3–4 tablespoons icing/
    confectioner's sugar
2 tablespoons sweet Marsala
    wine or cream
$\frac{1}{2}$ teaspoon rosewater

ALMOND SYRUP BISCUITS
450 g/1 lb. blanched almonds,
    toasted (see recipe introduction)
115 g/$\frac{1}{2}$ cup plus 1$\frac{1}{4}$ tablespoons
    golden caster/granulated sugar,
    plus 4 tablespoons for the syrup
grated zest and juice of 2 lemons
1 egg
plain/all-purpose flour,
    for rolling

TO SERVE
Almond Syrup Biscuits or other
    sweet biscuits/cookies
dates or sliced fruit, such as
    peaches, apricots or nectarines
pomegranate seeds (optional)

SERVES 6

Rosewater is sold in Middle Eastern stores and supermarket baking sections. If you can't find it, use Amaretto liqueur or vanilla. It's best to grind the almonds yourself, so they are fresher and have more texture (toast them first in a dry frying pan/skillet).

Preheat the oven to 180°C/fan 160°C/350°F/Gas 4 and line a baking sheet with baking paper.

To make the almond syrup cookies, put the toasted almonds into a food processor and grind to a coarse mixture. Transfer to a bowl, then add the sugar and lemon zest. Make a well in the centre, add the egg and mix well.

Transfer to a well-floured work surface and shape into a flat log, 25 x 7 x 1.5 cm/10 x 2$\frac{3}{4}$ x $\frac{5}{8}$ in. deep. Cut into 20–24 slices. Arrange apart on the prepared baking sheet, then bake in the preheated oven for 18 minutes. Remove from the oven and let cool on a wire rack.

Meanwhile, put the remaining 4 tablespoons sugar and the lemon juice into a saucepan and bring to the boil. Simmer for 3 minutes until syrupy. Let cool, then drizzle the mixture over the biscuits.

Put the mascarpone, icing/confectioner's sugar and Marsala or cream into a small heatproof bowl set over a saucepan of simmering water and heat, stirring until smooth. Stir in the rosewater. Transfer the mixture to a fondue pot set over its tabletop burner to keep warm. Serve with the almond syrup biscuits and fruit for dipping, and scatter over the pomegranate seeds, if using.

ORANGE & CARDAMOM FONDUE

1 tablespoon green cardamom
    pods
very finely grated zest of 1 large
    orange , plus 125 ml/½ cup
    freshly squeezed juice
2 egg yolks
1 egg
60 g/5 tablespoons caster/
    granulated sugar

CARAMEL GRAPES & DATES
250 g/9 oz. grapes
125 g/4½ oz. fresh or semi-dried
    dates
225 g/1 cup plus 2 tablespoons
    caster/granulated sugar

SERVES 4

This beautifully scented fondue is made using a method similar to zabaglione – it can be served in a fondue pot, or as individual servings in tea glasses or bowls.

Divide the grapes into small bunches and spear each date with a bamboo skewer. Put the sugar into a heavy-based saucepan, add 60 ml/4 tablespoons water and heat, stirring until the sugar has dissolved. Bring to the boil but do not stir – you can gently swirl the pan around so the sugar colours evenly. Boil for 5 minutes until the sugar is a golden caramel. Remove from the heat and, working quickly, dip bunches of grapes and dates into the caramel. Put onto a plate lined with baking paper, leave for the caramel to set, then transfer to small plates.

To prepare the fondue, put the cardamom into a dry frying pan/skillet and heat for 3 minutes until aromatic. Lightly crush the pods with a mortar and pestle. Put into a small saucepan, add the orange juice and zest and simmer gently for 2 minutes. Remove from the heat, let cool, then strain and measure 60 ml/4 tablespoons.

Put the egg yolks, egg and sugar into a heatproof bowl set over simmering water. Using electric beaters, whisk the mixture for 10 minutes until thick and mousse-like. Gradually whisk in the measured orange and cardamom mixture and continue whisking for 5 minutes. Pour into a fondue pot and set over its tabletop burner, or into individual glasses, then serve with the dates and grapes.

WHITE CHOCOLATE FONDUE

WITH LEMON & GIN

75 ml/5 tablespoons double/
   heavy cream
3 tablespoons gin
very finely grated zest of 2 lemons
225 g/8 oz. best-quality white
   chocolate, chopped

TO SERVE
500 g/1 lb. 2 oz. strawberries
250 g/9 oz. blueberries
sweet biscuits/cookies such
   as ladyfingers, madeleines,
   langues de chat or amaretti

SERVES 6

There are those who argue that white chocolate isn't 'real' chocolate. I don't think it matters – it's delicious and looks beautiful, and its sweet flavour marries perfectly with lemon and gin.

Wash the strawberries, but do not hull them, then pat them dry with kitchen paper (if you hull them before washing, they will fill with water). Thread a few blueberries onto small skewers. Arrange the blueberry skewers, strawberries and sweet biscuits/cookies on a serving plate.

Put the cream, gin and lemon zest into the top of a double boiler set over simmering water and heat gently. Add the chocolate and stir until smooth. Transfer to a fondue pot and set over its tabletop burner, then serve with the fruit and biscuits.

Note White chocolate is very thin when hot. If you would prefer a thicker fondue, turn off the burner, let cool, then chill for 1–2 hours before serving.

MALTED MILK S'MORES

325 g/11½ oz. milk chocolate, chopped
150 ml/⅔ cup single/light cream
1½ tablespoons malted milk powder
100 g/3½ oz. small marshmallows

SPECULOOS BISCUITS
300 g/2¼ cups plain/all-purpose flour
1 tablespoon ground mixed spice
1 teaspoon ground ginger
½ teaspoon baking powder
¼ teaspoon ground cinnamon
a pinch of freshly ground black pepper
100 g/7 tablespoons butter, diced
225 g/1 cup plus 2 tablespoons soft brown sugar
1 small egg, beaten

SERVES 4

Here's a great way to adapt a classic bonfire treat into a more formal dining experience. I loved malted milk as a child so its addition to the chocolate sauce is a touch nostalgic for me. I am particularly partial to speculoos biscuits (those little spiced cookies so often served in Europe with a cup of coffee) and they make a perfect dipper. The marshmallow-topped chocolate fondue can be grilled using raclette trays or, if you prefer, divide the fondue between individual dishes and use a conventional grill/broiler.

To make the biscuits/cookies, sift the flour, spices and pepper into a bowl until combined. Rub the butter into flour until the mixture resembles fine crumbs. Stir in the sugar and then gradually work in the egg and 2–3 teaspoons water to form a soft dough. Knead lightly into a ball, wrap in clingfilm/plastic wrap and refrigerate for 30 minutes.

Preheat the oven to 170°C/fan 150°C/325°F/Gas 3. Line 2 large baking sheets with baking paper.

Remove the dough from the fridge and roll on a lightly floured surface to form a log about 20 cm/8 in. long and 5 cm/2 in. in diameter. Start shaping the log into a flatter rectangle using a rolling pin and baking paper until it is about 3 cm/1¼ in. in height. Using a sharp knife, cut each piece of dough into 2-mm/⅛-in. thick biscuits and arrange on the prepared baking sheets leaving a 3-cm/1¼-in. gap between each one. Bake in the preheated oven for 15 minutes until lightly golden. Remove from the oven and transfer to a wire tray to cool completely. Store in an airtight container until required.

To make the fondue, place the chocolate, cream and malted milk powder in a small fondue pan and heat very gently, stirring until melted. Divide the mixture between the raclette trays or individual gratin dishes about 12 cm/5 in. in diameter. Diners can then add their marshmallows and pop them under the raclette grill (or a conventional grill/broiler) and cook until charred and gooey. Serve with the speculoos biscuits, sandwiching them together with the marshmallows if wished.

Note The biscuit recipe makes plenty, so keep any extra in an airtight container for up to a week.

CROÛTE CHOCOLAT

1 tablespoon butter, for greasing
400 g/14 oz. panettone, brioche or
    raisin bread (approx. 12 slices,
    about 10 cm/4 in. square and
    1.5 cm/³⁄₄ in. thick)
2 bananas, sliced
250 g/9 oz. strawberries, hulled
    and halved
60 ml/4 tablespoons amaretto
150 g/5¹⁄₂ oz. dark/bittersweet
    chocolate, grated
vanilla custard, to serve

SERVES 6

Bread and chocolate are a favourite, ever popular combination in Switzerland, and this sweet spin on the classic croûte fromage (see page 76) makes a great finale for any meal. Serve it with lashings of vanilla custard on the side.

Preheat the oven to 180°C/fan 160°C/350°F/Gas 4. Butter a 2-litre/quart baking dish.

Arrange the slices of panettone, brioche or raisin bread in overlapping rows in the prepared baking dish. Insert the slices of banana and strawberry halves between the slices of panettone. Sprinkle with amaretto and then add a layer of grated chocolate on top.

Transfer to the preheated oven and bake for 25 minutes, until puffed up and the chocolate has melted. Serve with plenty of vanilla custard.

INDEX

A
aligot 60
almonds: almond & basil dip 128
almond syrup biscuits 164
baharat spice mix 116
romesco sauce 41
anchovies: anchovy dressing 138
bagna cauda 124
Appenzeller fondue 22
apple rösti 54

B
baba buns 155
bacon: lobster, bacon, lobster & tomato toastie 72
goat's cheese rounds 99
tartiflette 67
bagna cauda 124
baharat spice mix 116
bananas: croûte chocolat 172
basil: almond & basil dip 128
pesto 59
Beaufort fondue 22
beef: beef with horseradish 141
fondue bourguignonne 115
Japanese beef 112
poached beef fillet 138
beer: blue cheese fondue 46
ploughman's fondue 18
queso fundido 21
beetroot/beets: beetroot & horseradish relish 141
goat's cheese bruschetta with roasted beetroot 88
berries: brûléed summer fruits with feta 100
frozen summer berries 156
biscuits: almond syrup biscuits 164
speculoos biscuits 171
black garlic & parsley pesto 60
blue cheese fondues 29, 46

blueberries: spiced blueberry relish 68
bok choy: poached Chinese chicken 133
bourbon: salted bourbon caramel sauce 159
bread: bacon, lobster & tomato toastie 72
croûte au fromage nature 76
croûte chocolat 172
goat's cheese bruschetta 88
Swiss fondue fritters 75
the ultimate cheese toastie 71
bread & butter pickles 71
breadsticks 14
walnut grissini 29
broths 133, 138, 142, 145
duck laksa broth 137
Indian-style broth 146
lemon-scented broth 134
poached Chinese chicken 133
saffron & tomato broth 149
brûléed summer fruits with feta 100
bruschetta, goat's cheese 88
burgers, Southern chicken 107
Burmese-style spiced pork 111
burners 9
butter, garlic & lemon 127

C
Cal-Mex baked garlic 92
calamari see squid
Calvados: Cheddar & Calvados fondue 54
caramel: caramel grapes & dates 167
caramelized orange sauce 155
salted bourbon caramel sauce 159
cardamom pods: orange & cardamom fondue 167
celeriac/celery root: poached beef fillet 138

skordalia 115
Champagne fondue 17
Cheddar & Calvados fondue 54
cheese fondues 6, 7, 11–33
see also raclette
cheesy melts 57–79
chestnuts: Comté with caramelized chestnuts 49
chicken: chicken & duck fondue 108
chicken in vine leaves 134
poached Chinese chicken 133
Southern chicken burgers 107
chillies/chiles: chilli oil 45
chilli sauce 120
jalapeño salsa 92
queso fundido 21
smoked chilli-chocolate fondue 160
tamarind sauce 111
tomato & onion jam 95
chimichurri sauce 123
Chinese pickles 45
chocolate: bitter chocolate fondue 163
croûte chocolat 172
malted milk s'mores 171
salted bourbon caramel sauce 159
smoked chilli-chocolate fondue 160
white chocolate custard 156
white chocolate fondue 168
chorizo sausages: queso fundido 21
churros 163
cider: Cheddar & Calvados fondue 54
cider fondue 25
cilantro see coriander
citrus dipping sauce 119
clams: Thai-style seafood steamboat 142
Comté fondue 22
Comté with caramelized chestnuts, raisins & hazelnuts 49

coriander/cilantro: chimichurri sauce 123
tomato & coriander salsa 21
corn, Tex-Mex grilled 96
court bouillon, Pernod 150
crab: ginger & crab fondue 53
croûte au fromage nature 76
croûte chocolat 172
cucumber: bread & butter pickles 71
crispy 5-spice tofu 120
fattoush salad 84
custard, white chocolate 156

D
dates: caramel grapes & dates 167
dips: almond & basil dip 128
citrus dipping sauce 119
mayonnaise dips 115
soy & sesame dipping sauce 133
doughnuts: churros 163
doughnuts with salted bourbon caramel 159
duck: chicken & duck fondue 108
duck laksa broth 137

E
electric fondues 7, 8

F
fattoush salad 84
fennel: cabbage, fennel & lime slaw 107
fish: Thai-style seafood steamboat 142
fondue bourguignonne 115
fondue Fribourgeois 22
fondue pans 8
fondue rolls with Taleggio 59
fondue Savoyarde 13
fonduta 30, 37
fries, polenta 123
fritters 75, 107

G

garlic: bagna cauda 124
  black garlic & parsley
    pesto 60
  Cal-Mex baked garlic 92
  garlic & lemon butter 127
  raclette over roasted
    potatoes, garlic &
    shallots 91
  tamarind sauce 111
gin, white chocolate fondue
  with 168
ginger: ginger & crab
  fondue 53
  Japanese pickles 112
goat's cheese & honey
  fondue 38
goat's cheese bruschetta
  88
goat's cheese rounds 99
grapes: caramel grapes &
  dates 167
green goddesss
  mayonnaise 145
green salsa 115
grissini, walnut 29

H

halloumi & fattoush salad
  84
ham: the ultimate cheese
  toastie 71
hollandaise, miso 112
honey: goat's cheese &
  honey fondue 38
horseradish: beetroot &
  horseradish relish 141
hotpots 6, 8, 142

J

jalapeño salsa 92
Japanese beef 112
Japanese pickles 112

L

laksa paste 137
lamb fondue 116
langoustine, poached 145
lemon: garlic & lemon
  butter 127
  lemon-scented broth 134
limes: cabbage, fennel &
  lime slaw 107

citrus dipping sauce 119
  green salsa 115
lobster: bacon, lobster &
  tomato toastie 72
  lobster & sole 150

M

malted milk s'mores 171
Marie Rose mayonnaise
  145
Marie Rose sauce 72
marshmallows: malted
  milk s'mores 171
mascarpone & rose fondue
  164
mayonnaise 145
  green goddesss
    mayonnaise 145
  Marie Rose mayonnaise
    145
  Marie Rose sauce 72
  mayonnaise dips 115
  Pernod mayonnaise 145
meringue kisses 156
miso hollandaise 112
modern fondues 35–55
monkfish: fish & seafood
  149
Mont d'Or with breadsticks
  14
mushrooms: pickled wild
  mushrooms 17
  poached Chinese chicken
    133
  porcini fonduta 37
mustard onions 79

N

Neuchâtel fondue 22
noodles: duck laksa broth
  137
  Thai-style seafood
    steamboat 142

O

oil, chilli 45
oil fondues 6, 8, 105–29
onions: mustard onions 79
  pickled red onion rings
    46
  tomato & onion jam 95
oranges: caramelized
  orange sauce 155

orange & cardamom
  fondue 167

P

pancetta: Reblochon
  pithivier 68
parsley: black garlic &
  parsley pesto 60
  chimichurri sauce 123
  green salsa 115
pastrami: croûte au
  fromage nature 76
peaches with raclette 103
peas: rasam with salmon
  146
pecans, caramelized 87
peppers (bell): chicken in
  vine leaves 134
  fattoush salad 84
  romesco sauce 41
Pernod court bouillon 150
Pernod mayonnaise 145
pesto 59
pickles: bread & butter
  pickles 71
  Chinese pickles 45
  Japanese pickles 112
  pickled red onion rings
    46
  pickled wild mushrooms
    17
pistachios: baharat spice
  mix 116
pithivier, Reblochon 68
pizza ring 64
ploughman's fondue 18
polenta/cornmeal fries 123
porcini fonduta 37
pork, Burmese-style spiced
  111
potatoes: apple rösti 54
  classic aligot 60
  classic raclette 83
  potato fries 46
  raclette over roasted
    potatoes 91
  skordalia 115
  tartiflette 67
  turmeric potatoes 146
prawns/shrimp: fish &
  seafood 149
  Thai-style seafood
    steamboat 142

prawn & calamari
  skewers 128
pretzels 25
pumpkin fondue 42

Q

queso fundido 21

R

raclette 7, 9, 81–103
radishes: Chinese pickles
  45
rasam with salmon 146
Reblochon pithivier 68
red cabbage: cabbage,
  fennel & lime slaw 107
relishes 68, 108, 141
romesco 41
rosé fondue 22
rösti, apple 54
rouille 149

S

saffron & tomato broth 149
salads: Dolcelatte & sweet
  potato salad with
  caramelized pecans 87
  fattoush salad 84
salmon: fish & seafood 149
  rasam with salmon 146
salsas: green salsa 115
  jalapeño salsa 92
  tomato & coriander salsa
    21
salted bourbon caramel
  sauce 159
scallops: fish & seafood
  149
  scallops with garlic &
    lemon butter 127
shallots, caramelized 33
shrimp see prawns
Sichuan fondue 45
skewers 8
  prawn & calamari
    skewers 128
skordalia 115
slaw: cabbage, fennel &
  lime 107
smoked fish fondues 50
s'mores, malted milk 171
sole: lobster & sole 150
sorrel: green salsa 115

soufflés, twice-baked cheese 63
Southern chicken burgers 107
soy & sesame dipping sauce 133
Spanish cheese fondue 41
speculoos biscuits 171
spice mix, baharat 116
squid/calamari: prawn & calamari skewers 128
    Thai-style seafood steamboat 142
steamboats 8, 142
stock fondues 6, 8, 131–51
strawberries: croûte chocolat 172
sweet fondues 153–73
sweet potatoes: Dolcelatte & sweet potato salad with caramelized pecans 87

sweetcorn cobs: Tex-Mex grilled corn 96
Swiss fondue fritters 75

T
tahini sauce 84
Taleggio & roasted vegetable wraps with tomato & onion jam 95
tamarind: rasam paste 146
    tamarind sauce 111
tartiflette 67
Tex-Mex grilled corn 96
Thai-style seafood steamboat 142
toasties: lobster, bacon & tomato toastie 72
    the ultimate cheese toastie 71
tofu: crispy 5-spice tofu 120
    duck laksa broth 137

tomatoes: lobster, bacon & tomato toastie 72
    roasted tomato fondue 26
    romesco sauce 41
    saffron & tomato broth 149
    sun-dried tomato & onion jam 95
    tomato & coriander salsa 21
    tomato & onion jam 95
    Tunisian relish 108
Tunisian relish 108
turmeric potatoes 146
twice-baked cheese soufflés 63

V
Vacherin fondue 33
vegetables: crispy vegetable fondue 119

Taleggio & roasted vegetable wraps with tomato & onion jam 95
vine leaves, chicken 134

W
waffles 160
walnut grissini 29
Welsh rabbit 79
wine 7
    Champagne fondue 17
    red wine & juniper stock 141
    rosé fondue 22
wraps: Taleggio & roasted vegetable wraps with tomato & onion jam 95

Y
yogurt: tahini sauce 84

RECIPE CREDITS

Recipes on pages 25, 26, 29, 30, 50, 53, 54, 79, 83, 108, 115, 116, 119, 124, 128, 134, 140, 149, 150, 163, 164, 167, 168 and 172 were originally published in 2002 in Fondue by Fiona Smith and adapted by Louise Pickford.

AUTHOR'S ACKNOWLEDGEMENTS

I would like to thank everyone at Ryland, Peters & Small for all their support and help in producing this book.